The complete book of cel   ⌐or
the appalachian dul   ⌐

by Mark Nelson

Audio Contents

1. Airde Chuain/The Clergy's Lamentation (4:25)
2. Trunkles/Haste to the Wedding (4:15)
3. Breton Wedding Tune/An Dro Arzh/An Dro Noalou (3:42)
4. The Bonnie Lass of Bon Accord (2:28)
5. The Aran Boat (3:39)
6. Another Jig Will Do/Jenny's Wedding/The Ships Are Sailing (3:53)
7. Oran Mór MacCleód/The Piobaireachd of Donald Ohu (5:54)
8. All Through the Night (4:20)
9. Sonny Brogan's Mazurka/Jackie Donnan's Mazurka (2:19)
10. Breton March/An Dro Boad/Breton March (Reprise) (5:18)
11. Sí Beg Sí Mór (The Faery Hills) (4:29)

Online Audio

www.melbay.com/95530BCDEB

Cover photo by Alan Mandell

1 2 3 4 5 6 7 8 9 0

© 1995, 2002 BY MEL BAY PUBLICATIONS, INC., PACIFIC, MO 63069.
ALL RIGHTS RESERVED. INTERNATIONAL COPYRIGHT SECURED. B.M.I. MADE AND PRINTED IN U.S.A.
No part of this publication may be reproduced in whole or in part, or stored in a retrieval system, or transmitted in any form or by any means, electronic, mechanical, photocopy, recording, or otherwise, without written permission of the publisher.

Visit us on the Web at www.melbay.com — E-mail us at email@melbay.com

This book is dedicated to good company,
good music and good cheer.....

Table of Contents

What is Celtic Music?

The Celts were a loosely organized group of Bronze Age peoples who lived across Europe— from Ireland and British Isles to France, Germany and Low Countries and all the way into the Balkans and even Turkey! Most of what we know of the Celts comes from the Romans, who were constantly bedeviled by these superb warriors who refused to behave like sensible civilized subjects. Over time, the tribes retreated to what are now regraded as the Celtic countries: mainly Ireland, Scotland, Britain and the northwest corner of France called Brittany.

The ancient Celts revered music (as do many of their modern day descendents); no old tale is complete without harpers and dancers, no battle took place but it was remembered in song. We can never know exactly what those mythic melodies sounded like; but listening to the keening of the pipes on a Scottish moor, or hearing a plaintive *sean nós* ballad, or dancing a wild Breton circle dance certainly brings us closer in spirit.

Celtic music and the Appalachian Dulcimer seem to go together. There's something in the drones and the sliding ornamentation that makes a Scot's air even more plaintive when played on the dulcimer. An Irish harp tune sounds as fresh today as it did in the great hall of an Eighteenth Century manor. And a Breton *plin* fits the familiar fingerboard as if it were a native.

The first people to discover the wonderful synergy of Celtic music and dulcimers were the unknown Scotch-Irish hill people of Appalachia who took a modest little German instrument, twisted and poked and prodded it into it's current shape, and applied their age-old repertoire to this "sweet voiced thing".

Some of the songs changed less in America over the ensuing years than they did in the home countries; others took on new names and a new, American accent. So *Miss McCleod's Reel* became *Hop High, Ladies*; *Pigtown Fling* became *Wild Horse at Stony Point*, and *The Chorus Jig* became a reel! Along the way, we Americans straightened out the galloping rhythm of the hornpipe and added a shuffle and a backbeat to everything else.

Today a new generation of dulcimer players is returning to the source to learn the fiddle, pipe and harp tunes played in the Celtic lands. Celtic music has proven to be remarkably adaptable; adding and discarding instruments easily over the years--the fiddle is essentially an Italian invention, accordions and concertinas came from Germany in the 19th Century, and the Irish banjo comes from America by way of Africa. So why not a Celtic dulcimer?

Here, then, is a book to help you along the way. You will notice that it concentrates on instrumental music; after much long and hard thought it seemed that this would give the best overview of Celtic styles. Besides, there is a lovely old tradition of playing vocal pieces instrumentally as slow airs--properly done, it will send chills up your spine. So included here are a number of songs, both common and obscure, for you to play on your dulcimer.

The bulk of the material is dance music, because this is what you will hear played at sessions wherever Celtic musicians gather. These are the same tunes, in the same keys, as played by fiddlers, accordionists, whistlers and more...now all that's left is to gather some friends, tune up, and move back the kitchen furniture for a good old fashioned *ceili*.

Acknowledgments

In many ways, this book began over twenty-five years ago, before anybody told me it was impossible to play Celtic music on the Appalachian dulcimer. Luckily, there were lots of other dulcimer players who failed to get the word, and so we were able to share tunes and create a new vocabulary for this deceptively simple little instrument. So raise a glass to Holly Tannen, Kent Steadman, Lori Cole, Bonnie Carol, David Snaufer, Larkin Bryant, Neal Helman, Peter Tommerup, Jake Walton, Roger Nicholson, Leo Kretzner, Michael Rugg, and all the rest!

Many people helped this book take its present form; the following deserve my sincere thanks:

Danny Carnahan and Chris Caswell for supplying reams of hard to find material and generous help with stylistic niceties.

Lance Frodsham for allowing me to use his arrangement of *Dans Mod Koh a Vaod*.

Jamie Haggerty for *Jabadaw* and general dulcimic inspiration over the years.

Jocelyn Reynolds for piles really silly British tunes. I'm still waiting for our all dog Morris team—Ruby and Cosmo already have the sticks...

William Bay for suggesting the book in the first place.

Many thanks to the many, many musicians here and abroad who have generously shared tunes over the years; with special appreciation for Nick the fiddler in Cornwall (I wonder, did you ever get the donkey?), Joe O'Dowd, Kevin Burke, Robin Petrie, Brian Freeman, Kathy Moore, Mickie Zekley, Mark Jardine, and at least one of the many Seamus Egans.

And thanks to Annie, who thinks it's a lot nicer around the house since I quit trying to play the accordion.

Index of Tunes

Irish

Scottish

Harp Tunes & Airs

British

Breton

About the music

Sources

The majority of the tunes come from three sources: harp music, the piper's repertoire and fiddle tunes. The fiddle is probably the most popular instrument in Ireland and Scotland, and there are truly incredible numbers of tunes associated with it. Even though the fiddle and the dulcimer have pretty much the same range, playing a fiddle tune on the dulcimer may require some work to get all of the notes to fit. But the extra effort is always worth it--Celtic fiddle tunes sound great on the dulcimer.

Although some harp tunes are ancient, most of the melodies loved by dulcimer players date from the late 17th and early 18th centuries. According to the few contemporary sources, the Celtic harpers of old employed complex ornamentation, difficult descending arpeggios and great melodic variation in their playing. The majority of the harp tunes we have available to us were written by the celebrated Irish composer Turlough O'Carolan (1670-1738). While drawing on the centuries-old harp tradition, Carolan was none the less influenced by the Italian Baroque music popular among his patrons. You might want to take that into consideration when playing his tunes; nothing sounds finer than adding fancy trills and simple counterpoint to suggest the sound of an opulent drawing room.

People usually think of the bagpipe as the national instrument of Scotland, but in fact, the large *Highland* pipes are but one of many kinds of bagpipes played in Celtic lands. In the north west of France, the Breton *binou*, a sweet-sounding little bagpipe, and *bombarde,* a raucous oboe-like instrument, typically play for dances; while Ireland is home to an intricate contraption known as the *Uilleann* or Union pipes. All bagpipes share certain characteristics: a greatly reduced scale, the use of complex ornamentation to differentiate between unstopped notes, and the use of drones. Bagpipe tunes seem to translate particularly well to the Appalachian dulcimer, especially when it is tuned to a unison or *Bagpipe* tuning!

Broadly speaking, the tunes can be grouped as well along national and regional lines. Granted, there is an enormous overlap among the countries usually called the British Isles; but even when playing the identical tune, an Irish or Scottish musician will somehow make the melody sound unique.

The Breton repertoire is a little different; the music is characterized by shifting time signatures and an unusual interplay between the two instruments that make up the traditional ensemble. Typically, the *binou* plays the entire tune, with the *bombarde* weaving in and out, overlapping certain phrases, omitting others. Although a few melodies appear to be shared with Cornish and Welsh traditions, the majority are either native or are naturalized adaptations of Medieval church music or even modern French folksongs. Breton tunes are just beginning to make their way on to the dulcimer; this representative sampling is just the beginning.

Astute scholars of Celtic lore will notice that entire traditions have been left out or scarcely represented. This was not intended as a slight; rather the styles chosen are those most likely to be encountered on recordings, in concert, and in sessions.

Glossary of Styles

The tunes can be roughly broken down as follows:

Reels are in 2/4 and 4/4 time and are usually played pretty fast. In fact, fiddlers in sessions have taken to playing both reels and jigs at tempos far faster than usual for dancers. Feel free to slow them down a little.

Jigs, with their swingy triple feel, are the quintessential Irish rhythm (The *Irish Washerwoman* is a jig). Jigs can be further broken down into:

Hornpipes, like reels, are in duple or quadruple meter. Usually played slower than reels, the hornpipe has a particular galloping rhythm sometimes notated as:

It is easier to read a hornpipe written with eighth notes; just remember to give the tune a swing when you play it. Throughout this book, you will see the notation ♪♪ = ♪.♪ to remind you to play with the proper feel.

Strathspeys are a unique form of reel from the Northeast of Scotland (the name means "Valley of the River Spey"). Characterized by dotted rhythms, Strathspeys are the favorite of fiddlers everywhere for their challenging right hand bowing patterns. Play them more slowly than reels, and emphasize their unique rhythms.

Polkas, while not native to the Celtic countries, enjoy a great popularity. Play them as fast as you can.

The **mazurka**, which sounds something like a fast waltz, is another import. The two included here are great fun to play.

Slides are a very fast jig-type tune from Ireland's County Kerry. They are written either as 6/8 or 12/8; either way, play them with spirit.

Marches were played to keep soldiers in step; now they are better used to help brides and grooms reach the altar on time. Celtic marches tend to have a feel that alternates between double and triple meter no matter how they are written.

Piobaireachds are a peculiar form of ancient Scottish pipe music. Like all music written for bagpipes, they contain complex, formalized ornamentation of grace notes played above and below some melody notes.

Set Dances are those tunes associated with a particular dance. They can be jigs, hornpipes, or reels. Set dance tunes often depart from the strict rule of playing each section of the tune two times through, and may have sections of unequal length.

Airs are usually slow melodies played for dramatic effect. As much a style as a type of tune, airs tend to be highly ornamented and feature an almost vocal playing style. Since the word "air" literally means "melody", any tune the doesn't fit into any other category can be considered an air. What's more, you can take any tune, slow it down, and call it an air.

Planxties are tunes written by the harper Turlough O'Carolan for his many patrons. No one knows quite what the word means, although "in praise of" or "to the health of" are good guesses.

Country Dance music embraces a wide variety of English and Scottish dances in several meters, including reels, hornpipes, jigs and waltzes, as well as the aptly-named rant.

Morris Dancing is traditionally done for holidays in various parts of the British Isles. The tunes are usually similar to reels, jigs, hornpipes, etc., often with the addition of a section played in free meter to accompany the capers, or leaps, of the dancers. Purists may question the inclusion of Morris and other British tunes in a book of Celtic music; but the melodies and structure show great affinity to Irish and Scottish music and they are fun to play. The author assumes full responsibility for any harm that may be done to the folklorically sensitive by their inclusion herein.

As mentioned before, **Breton** tunes are in something of a class by themselves. For one thing, the Breton tradition tended to be highly fragmented within the overall region, with particular tunes and dances associated with each village and community. Pipers from one area would refuse to play tunes from a neighboring town; likewise the same melody or dance would be known by many different names. Often the tune or dance is named after the place it came from. Needless to say, this can cause more than a little confusion. There has been a wonderful renaissance of Breton music and culture in the past few years, and so it is getting easier to hear this haunting music.

Some of the different dances include **An Dro, Plin,** and **Jabadaw** (all 4/4), **Laridenn** (either 3/4 or 4/4) and the **Dans Mod Koh (a Voad)** which shifts between 4/4 and 3/4. There are many, many others. One common characteristic is the linking of several related tunes into a suite, which is then usually played in a set order.

One characteristic of folk music is the existence of many different versions of the same song. As melodies get passed on from player to player, across borders and across time, it is only natural that changes subtle and dramatic will creep in. (For a good example of how this works, see the odd version of Turlough O'Carolan's *Princess Royal* as played for Morris dancers!) Keep in mind as you learn these tunes that each represents one unique setting among many. Sometimes the most common version has been chosen; others are a little more rare.

Although the music is arranged by country of origin, many of these melodies are common to more than one tradition. Feel free to mix and match them as you go.

How to Read Tablature

All of the music is written in standard notation and tablature for a dulcimer with three courses of strings. (If your dulcimer is set up with four equidistant strings, simply tune one of them as an extra drone.) Tunings appear at the beginning of each tune. Some of the tunes require an extra, or 6 1/2, fret, most do not.

Tablature, or TAB, is a ancient system of musical notation where lines represent the instrument's strings and the fingering positions are indicated by numbers. In the following example, the bottom line is the melody or treble string (or strings, if your dulcimer has doubled melody strings), the middle line represents the middle string, and the top line is the bass. The letters tell you how to tune each string:

The numbers tell you which fret to play, with 0 being the unfretted, or open string, 1 the first fret, 2 the second and so on. Here's a G major scale:

Since some strings are left blank, it is up to you whether to play them as drones (open strings) or to avoid them all together. It has become common when writing dulcimer TAB to leave off notating drone strings so the page doesn't get cluttered up with a bunch of zeros.

TAB doesn't give any indication of how long to hold each note; for that refer to the staff above the TAB.

Notice that here the TAB numbers correspond with the notes on the staff; if you are unfamiliar with standard musical notation see the next section.

Since each player develops a personal style, fingerings have not been indicated. Generally, the exact fingering will be determined by what is going on in the tune. So for the opening of *Morpath Rant* try using your ring, middle and index fingers in series:

Joe O'Dowd's Jig uses the first and second fingers to hold the outside strings at the same fret while the thumb plays much of the melody:

Experiment with different fingerings to see what works best for you. Ornaments such as hammer-ons, pull-offs and slides are rarely included—that's for each player to add. Remember that the way to play Celtic music is to slightly vary the melody each time it comes around.

If a string is left blank, that usually means you can play it as a drone or not; the choice is yours. The only exception would be when the open string would clash with the melody. Sometimes you can fill in the chords that are implied in the TAB.

For example, this figure:

```
    D  1
T A      2
A
B D        0
```

could be played like this:

```
    D  1        1
T A    2  2    2
A
B D  0        0
```

So let your ears be your guide. Of course, sometimes the dissonance is just the thing to make the hair stand up on the back of your head!

You may find flatpicking the faster tunes is the way to go, playing only the notes indicated and grabbing the occasional drone off of an adjacent string. Harp tunes and other airs sound wonderful when fingerpicked—use the TAB and the chord symbols as a guide in creating your own arrangement.

Generally, the best way to approach the tab is as a roadmap, once you know the basic melody feel free to explore. It's only when these melodies get off of the page and into your fingers that they begin to live.

About the Keys

In the old days, the music was sung in whatever key fit the singer's range. An instrumental tune was played in the key the instrument played in, whatever that may be, and there was no problem. When people began to try to play together, things got a little more complicated, and certain standards developed. But these *standard* keys still depend on which instruments are being used! So fiddles tend to play in the sharp keys of G, D, and A (and all of their relative modes); Breton pipes play in the flat keys-mostly F, Bb and Eb and *their* relative modes. And melodeons play in whatever key they happen to be made in, with C, G and D being the most common.

The fiddle tunes in this book are in the keys that fiddle players usually play them in. Since most dulcimer players are familiar with tuning into sharp keys, this shouldn't pose much of a challenge. (By the way, a couple of tunes got transposed so they'd fit the dulcimer better. There you go...)

Harp pieces are now generally played in sharp keys, although Bunting notated them mostly in flat keys 'way back in 1789. Some appear here in the keys contemporary harpers play them, others are transposed to make them easier to play on the dulcimer. The same goes for pipe tunes and airs.

The Breton repertoire seems to be quite flexible as to key, so take these settings as examples and feel free to transpose as you see fit.

Tuning and Transposition

As befits a folk instrument with a long history, there are numerous ways to tune the Appalachian dulcimer. Some people play their entire lives in only one or two tunings; some pride themselves in developing unique tunings for each song.

The important thing to remember is not to confuse *tuning* with *key*---it is possible to play in several different keys in any given dulcimer tuning. (It is beyond the scope of this book to dig too deeply into this subject. If you feel you need more information, consult any good dulcimer instruction book.) Dulcimer tunings tend to fall into a few categories based on the relationships between the strings. Generally the tonic is on the bass string or the middle string and the melody string is tuned to provide the correct mode, or you employ some combination of stopped strings to fool the dulcimer into playing into a related key.

So, for example, all *Mixolydian*, (sometimes called 1-5-8, or I-V-I) tunings are identical as far as how you finger them. So a tune written in D-A-D tuning can easily be transposed up a half step by retuning to Eb-Bb-Eb to get in tune with a fixed pitch instrument.

The process can be taken one step further by moving a tune from one string to another. Say you want to transpose *Breton March* from the key of D minor to A minor. One way would be just to raise all of your strings a fourth, from D-A-C to A-E-G. But the chances are you'd pop a wire before you got near those pitches. A better way might be to put the melody on the middle string tuned down to G and use the two outside strings as drones. Slacken the bass string to A while raising the treble to E, giving you A-G-E. You can now play the exact same fingering as before, only you play the tune on the middle string instead of the melody string. Of course, the pitches would be different, but that's the whole point.

It is very common for Celtic musicians to play related tunes together as medleys, often moving between relative major and minor modes. Try to find tunes that share a tuning, then string them together. You might put together *Off She Goes, The Joys of My Life* and *The Kid on the Mountain* since they are all played in D-A-D tunings. But the tunes are in the keys of D major, G major and E minor, which might make for an exciting arrangement!

Alternately, you may try transposing some tunes to take advantage of different harmony possibilities or to fit them into a medley. The music will reward your experimentation---that's how it has lasted all these years!

Reading Musical Notation

Folk music has been around far longer than writing, so it really isn't necessary to know how to read music in order to enjoy these tunes. If you already have a pretty good idea of how a tune is supposed to sound, either from hearing it on a recording or from repeated exposure at sessions you can jump in and figure it out from the TAB. But some knowledge of standard notation will greatly enhance your enjoyment of the book.

The best way to approach written music is to think of it as a map. Just like roads and rivers and buildings are represented schematically on a roadmap, so are the twists and turns of a well-made tune represented graphically on the staff. If you can use an atlas to find Loch Ness, then you can learn to find your way around a simple fiddle tune on paper.

Since the TAB will give you the correct pitches on a properly tuned dulcimer, you really only have to worry about the rhythm of a particular piece. Fortunately, there are clues.

The first clue is what looks like a fraction at the left hand side of the page. The top number tells you how many beats there are in each measure; the bottom number refers to the kind of note that gets the beat. (More on that in a minute.)

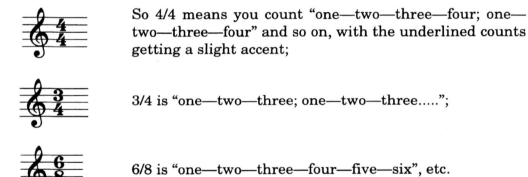

So 4/4 means you count "one—two—three—four; one—two—three—four" and so on, with the underlined counts getting a slight accent;

3/4 is "one—two—three; one—two—three.....";

6/8 is "one—two—three—four—five—six", etc.

Sometimes you may see additional symbols as well. Cut Time (¢) is another way of writing 2/2; and Common Time (**C**) is the same as 4/4.

Each beat can be further divided into smaller and smaller bits; which gets us to note values:

o   The longest note is the whole note; it gets held for four counts.

𝅗𝅥   Next comes the half note, with a value of two counts.

♩   The quarter note gets one count.

An eighth note is 1/2 as long as a quarter. How do you count less than one beat? Say "one—and-two—and—three—and—four—and—"

 The sixteenth note is half as long as the eighth note; so two sixteenths equal one eighth, four sixteenths equal a quarter, and sixteen equal a whole note.

There are also ways to tell you when not to play, and for how long. These are called rests, and they correspond to each of the different note values.

$$o = - \qquad \textstyle\frac{1}{2} = - \qquad \textstyle\frac{1}{4} = \xi \qquad \eighth = \gamma \qquad \sixteenth = \gamma$$

A dot placed next to a note (or rest) lengthens it by one half of its value. For example:

$$\textstyle\frac{1}{2}. = \eighth\eighth\eighth \qquad \eighth. = \sixteenth\sixteenth\sixteenth$$

You find dotted rhythms all over the place in Scottish music.

Ties are used for notes that are held for their combined values:

This figure would be held for three counts.

Finally, the triplet is a group of three notes that are played in the space of two.

For example, three eighth note triplets

would be played in the same amount of time as two eighth notes:

There are a few other marks to help you find your way around:

These special brackets, called repeat signs, tells you to repeat the enclosed phrase one time before going on to the next one. (Note that often only the final repeat sign is shown. This is a convention of writing folk tunes; treat it just as if the first sign was there.)

 This sign means play the measures under the sign on the first time through and then go back to the beginning of the section. On the repeat you skip over the first ending and play the second ending.

D.C.	From the Italian, Da Capo, meaning "Head". This sign directs you to go back to the beginning of the music.
D.S.	Dal Segno, or "to the sign", tells you to look for the symbol (𝄋) and play that section next rather than returning to the beginning.
⌢	A fermata is the symbol to hold a note just a little longer than its value. It is used to add expression to your playing.

In order for the music to fit onto the staff without the use of lots of ledger lines, the actual pitches played on the dulcimer may be an octave higher or lower than what is written. This is a fairly standard way to write music for instruments like the guitar, fiddle and dulcimer.

Learning to read music is like learning another language. At first everything seems incomprehensible, but gradually you are able to pick up a word here and a phrase there. Just about any good basic music theory book can help you get started reading music, but there really is no substitute for thoughtful practice. As you work through the arrangements in this book, think about how the notes relate to your dulcimer and its tunings. Notice how the different rhythms sound when you play them. It won't be long before you will begin to see how these simple building blocks can have tremendous expressive power.

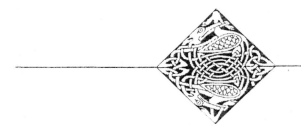

How to play Celtic Music

The majority of the tunes in this book can be played for dances, since this was one of the main traditional uses of music in the old days. Among Celtic dance tunes, the most common form is a melody of four or eight measures which repeats once, followed by a related melody of equal length, which also repeats. That form can notated as **A A B B**, with **A** being the first strain and **B** the second. You will notice that each section is in turn made up of smaller divisions, which often repeat in predictable ways.

For example, let's look at the first section of *The Soldier's Joy,* a tune common to Irish, Scottish and North American fiddle repertoires:

If you look at the 1st, 3rd and 5th measures, you'll see that they are exactly the same. That sure cuts down on the amount of material you have to learn! You may also notice that the first eight measures seem to break down into two equal halves.

Let's add the second part:

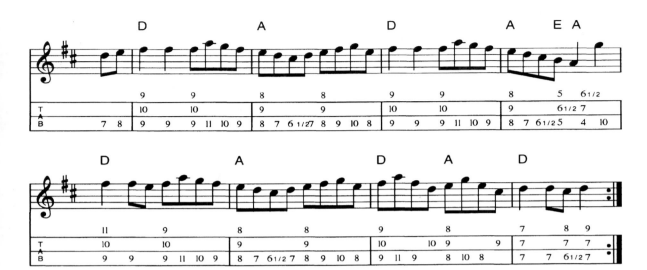

Notice anything? That's right, there is the same pattern of repeated measures as before. What's more, it looks as if the last measure of the **A** section is the same as the last measure of the **B** section.

There is a reason for all of this repetition. Remember that all music was learned by ear until relatively recently. So it makes sense to break tunes down into easily remembered little sections. You can use that to your advantage in learning these tunes; rather than tackling the entire piece at once, learn the tune phrase by phrase. That will make your job easier, and it will put the proper kind of breathing into your playing.

Another thing common to Celtic music is that most traditional musicians will follow the dance structure, taking all of the repeats in their proper place, even when there are no dancers present. It's a good idea to get into this habit right from the beginning so you can join into a session where ever you go.

One last thing; there are always exceptions to every rule, and there are legions of tunes that don't do what you expect them to. That's part of the fun.

Regional Styles & Ornamentation

One of the characteristics of Celtic art is an ornate kind of interwoven surface decoration; animal forms, plants and ornamental braiding weave into complex knots twisting around and in on themselves until the eye gets lost in the complexity. The most famous example is the Book of Kells, an ancient Irish manuscript of stunning beauty.

In a similar way, the Celtic musician takes a simple melodic line and weaves it in and around itself; adding ever more complex ornamentation with each pass. In fact, it is often the kinds of ornaments used that differentiate between otherwise identical melodies from different countries. There are countless regional variations; and of course each instrument has its own unique types of ornamentation. Furthermore, individuals may choose to decorate a tune differently depending on whether it is played for listening or dancing....The point here is that it is the ornamentation that makes Celtic music come alive.

Broadly speaking, **Irish** music tends to be more highly ornamented than other Celtic music; the Irish musician will add grace notes, triplets, slurs, and every other trick in the book to give life to the tune—but the essential melody will always shine through. When playing an Irish tune, be sure to emphasize the upbeats rather than the downbeat; this gives life to the music. You may notice a similarity between Irish music and American jazz, both are played with a lilting swing that is almost impossible to put into words.

This is particularly important when playing hornpipes; although a tune may be notated like this:

It actually sounds more like this:

To a lesser extent, this bouncy rhythm works for reels, jigs and other Irish styles as well.

There are numerous ways to add ornaments to Irish music, here are a few examples that work particularly well on the dulcimer:

22

Triplets can be inserted wherever you think you can get away with them. One way is with a quick hammer-on, pull-off combination:

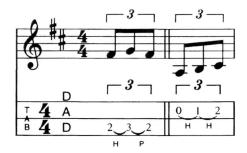

Another is done with a fast triplet strum by the picking hand.

The **cut** is a grace note one or more scale degrees above the melody, done very quickly.

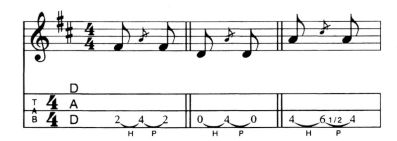

Rolls are combinations of grace notes that fall both above and below the note to be emphasized.

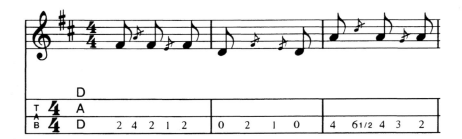

Remember to play the grace notes very rapidly!

One important note is to realize that a good player never plays the tune two times through exactly the same way; in fact, you may never play the tune exactly as it is written once you've learned it! Remember, the written music is only a guide.

Here are a couple of examples of how you might "read" a tune to employ different variations.

Replace quarter notes with triplets. Here's the first two bars of *Morrison's Jig* as written:

And with a triplet roll:

Or you can vary the melody slightly. This phrase from *Tobin's Favorite:*

Can be played like this:

Slow Airs present a special case— the player may attempt to capture all of the complex nuances of an impassioned vocal performance. Strict tempo is the exception; notes will be held for emphasis, phrases elongated or compressed at will. You can use every trick you can think of, including classical sounding arpeggios, trills and glissandos.

There are many, many more ways to vary a tune. The best way to learn is to listen to lots and lots of Irish music played by master musicians.

Scottish fiddle music tends to feature more intricate right hand bowing parts over actual ornaments and grace notes. Try bringing out the snap of a Strathspey using a flick of the pick. Some dulcimer players find it easier to get the complex rhythms of a Strathspey by fingerpicking. Whatever style you chose, be sure to play with a vibrant authority.

Certain Scottish tunes are designed to be played more slowly than their Irish cousins. Composed tunes like *The Bonnie Lass of Bon Accord* and *Princess Augusta* have an almost stately grace.

The Highland bagpipe has its own highly developed form of ornamentation and gracing that lends that instrument much of its special character. For example, here's what a bagpipe tune looks like to a piper:

For simplicity's sake, pipe tunes in this book are written without the grace notes, but you may want to try to add you own.

Here are a few examples of how to approximate bagpipe ornamentation on a dulcimer. Try using rapid combinations of hammer-ons and pull-offs to play the grace notes. Once again, there is no substitution for listening and experience.

Play **English** tunes with a strong emphasis on the downbeat. While Irish music is known for a lilting quality, English tunes are solidly down to earth. One of the features of a Morris Dance set is the *capers,* where the dancers leap into the air. The musician's role is to slow the tune down to match the cadence of the dancer, and then resume tempo for the next section. You will notice the tunes may imply a rhythmic change, either with a *fermata* (⌢) or by shifting into a different rhythm.

This is an example of the transition into a capers section. Notice how the pulse changes from quarter notes to half notes.

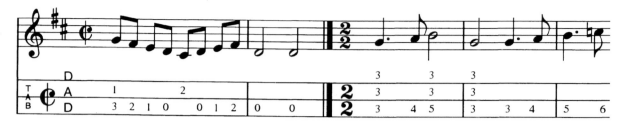

Play the capers sections freely to contrast with the regular beats of a standard dance tune. One of the keys to playing English tunes is to remember that the music moves in time to the dancers' feet. So you may want to picture someone leaping into the air on each long note—hold the note a little longer than you would normally, then speed up again to prepare for the next leap. Once you get the hang of it, it's a lot of fun.

Most of the **Breton** music included here comes from the piper's repertoire. Again, use hammer-ons, pull-offs and slides to mimic the complex piper's figures. For example, you can add quick grace notes and turns like this:

One characteristic of Breton music is the interplay between the two main instruments, the *binou* and the *bombarde*. Typically, the *binou* will play the tune through without stopping, while the *bombarde* weaves in and out; emphasizing part of a phrase here, another here. If you play with someone else, you can create a similar effect. One person plays the tune all the way through, the other plays every other phrase or section. It takes a little practice to find where to start and stop; often the *bombarde* will start on the final note of a phrase and play through to the next strong beat!

As you get into the Breton music, you can't help but notice the complex shifting of time signatures—two measures of 6/8 followed by one of 15/8 ?! Just remember to try each tune slowly until you get familiar with it. Of course, listening to as much Breton music as you can will help. Notice that all the shifting around of time signatures often give the piece a walking or breathing quality.

Harmony

Traditionally, Celtic music was played with little or no harmony. Solo performances were the norm, or groups of instruments would play a kind of polyglot unison, each adding ornaments to the same basic tune. Many of the older modal tunes don't fit into usual harmonic arrangements.

Such harmony as there was usually took the form of drones; usually on the tonic and fifth, but sometimes on the fourth, third, or second! Irish *Uilleann* pipers can add additional accompaniment through the use of the regulators; stringed instrument players may add one or more unstopped strings. You might try adding notes on an adjacent string to simulate the sound of the pipes; or pick out open strings in various combinations. Use your ear to decide if it works; if it doesn't sound good, try something else.

Try playing *The Duke of Fife* as written with drones:

Now add some extra notes on the middle string:

It has become common in recent years to accompany Celtic music with chords played on a guitar tuned to D A D G A D or some other "open" tuning, using suspensions and elaborate chord substitutions to suggest harmony without locking the music down to a particular major/minor key. Movable chord forms found in these tunings often impart a wonderful counterpoint to the movement of the melody.

You can create a similar effect on your dulcimer by playing simple little moving lines in parallel thirds or fifths on two strings, while maintaining a drone on an open string. Here's a harmonized D major scale; notice that the harmony is slightly different whether you are going up the scale or coming down:

		D															
T	A		3	4	5	6	7	8	9	10	10	9	8	7	6	5	4	3
B	D		2	3	4	5	7	7	8	9	9	8	9	7	5	4	4	2

27

You can use any, or all, of the following figures as substitutions for D major chords:

D

	D				
T A	3	4	5	7	10
B D	2	3	4	7	9

G chords:

	D				
T A	1	3	6	8	10
B D	0	3	5	7	10

And A chords:

	D			
T A	0	4	4	9
B D	1	1	4	8

Em:

	D			
T A	1	4	6	8
B D	1	3	5	8

Bm:

	D			
T A	1	3	5	8
B D	2	2	5	9

It is a simple matter to create interesting, moving harmonies from very simple building blocks. A little practice will reward you will many other chordal ideas, and other dulcimer tunings will give still more possibilities.

As stated earlier, many tunes don't really fall into our usual notions of harmony, which leaves them pretty much open to experimentation. One notorious example is the Irish jig *The Blarney Pilgrim*. Is it in D? Or G? The truth is, it doesn't _really_ fit in either key; either set of chords will work, more or less. This book chooses to harmonize the tune in the key of G; tuning the dulcimer so the drones play the tonic and the fifth of a G chord. You may find other versions that use the exact same pitches, but harmonize them with chords in the D major family and tune the dulcimer so the drones are D and A. Which one is right? That's for you to choose.

With the introduction of new instruments such as the piano, accordion, and guitar, modern harmonic ideas began to get superimposed upon the older forms. Sometimes the melodies would be changed to more nearly fit "classical" harmony; often new tunes would be written to take advantage of the new ideas. Some tunes, notably O'Carolan harp pieces and many of J. Scott Skinner's fiddle showstoppers, cry out for the full-fledged classical harmonic treatment. All of this is a long-winded way of saying that almost anything goes when harmonizing Celtic music. Each arrangement in this book is but one of many different harmonic interpretations; there are always other ways of doing it.

When all is said and done, the best way to play Celtic music is straight from the heart. So listen to everyone you can, and absorb a little from each. Then tune up your dulcimer and start playing....

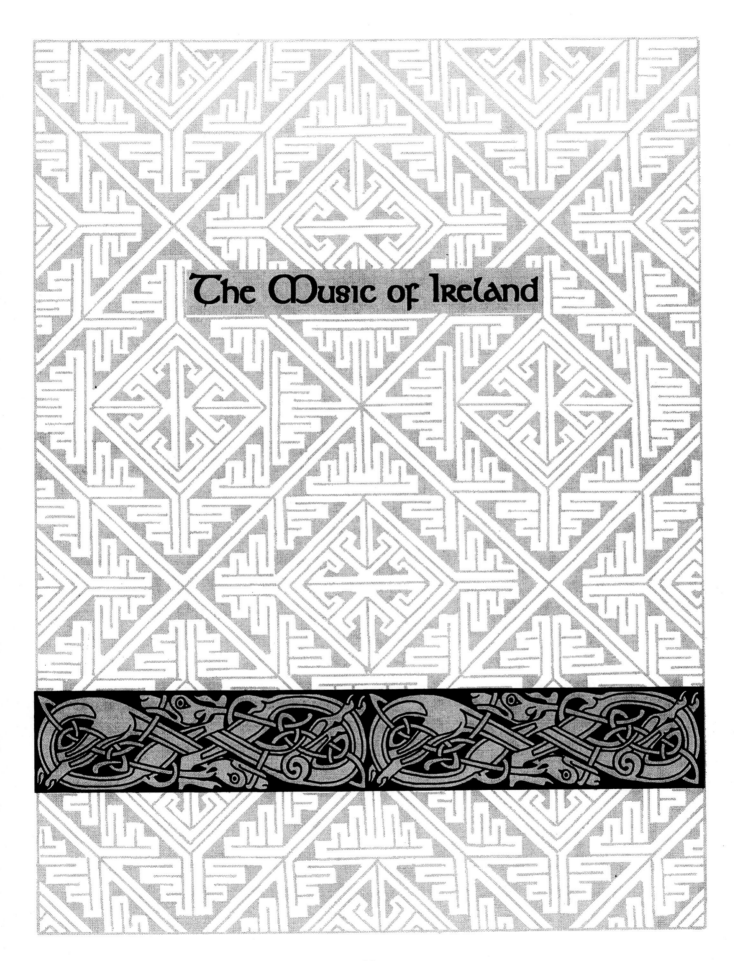

The Music of Ireland

The Rose in the Heather
Jig

The Frost is All Over
Jig

Haste to the Wedding
Jig

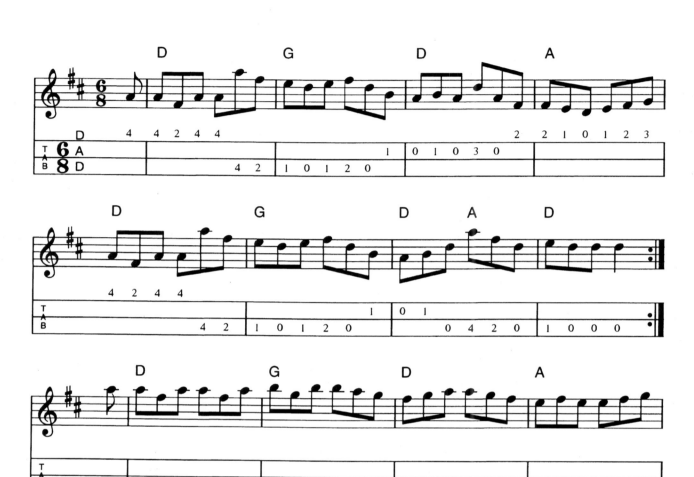

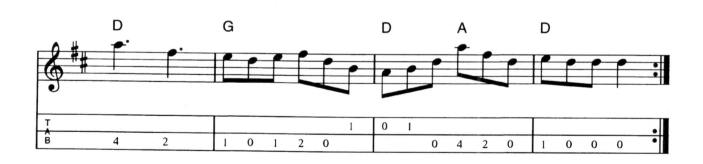

The Connachtman's Rambles
Jig

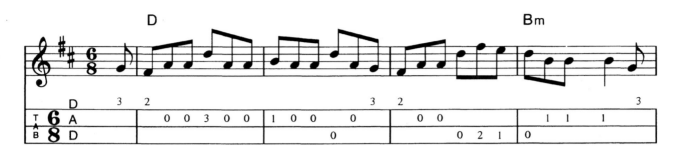

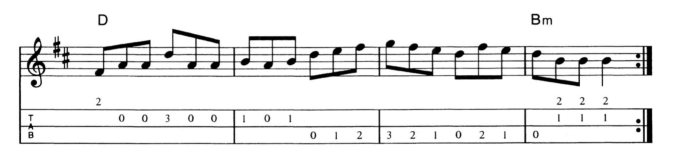

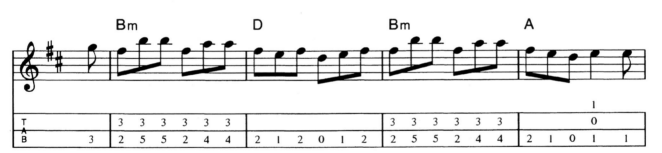

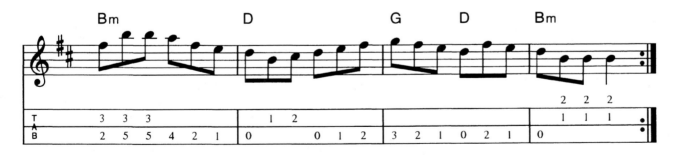

Smash the Windows
Single Jig

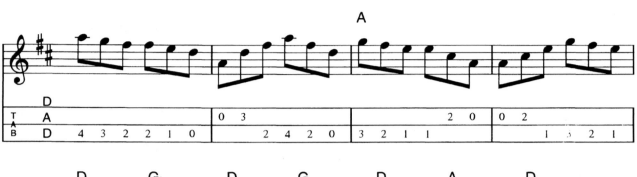

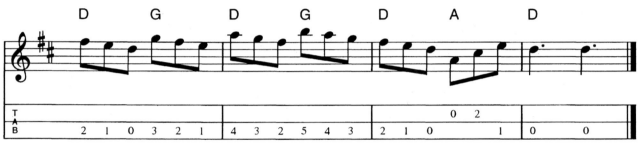

Off She Goes
Single Jig

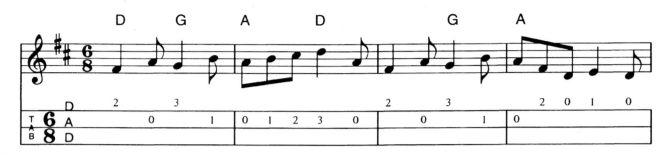

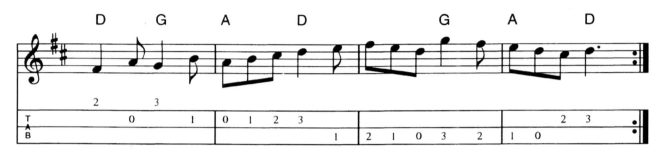

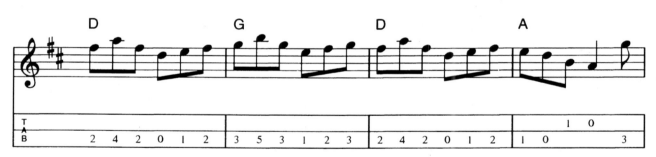

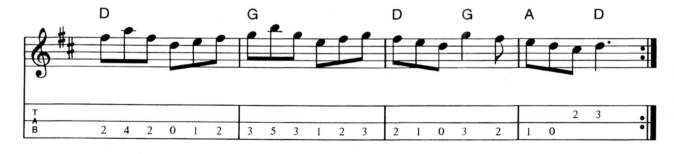

Tobin's Favorite

Jig

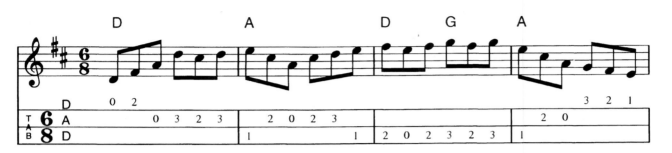

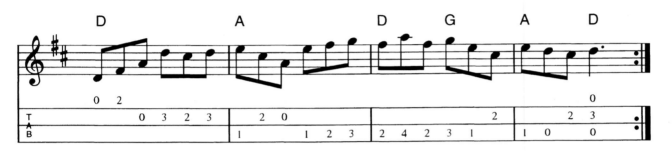

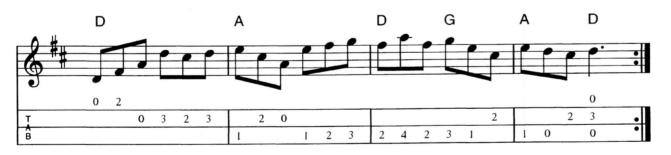

Morrison's Jig

The Joys of My Life
(Donnybrook Fair)
Jig

The Blarney Pilgrim
Jig

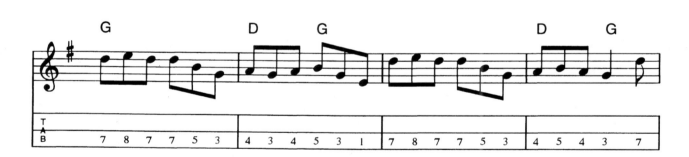

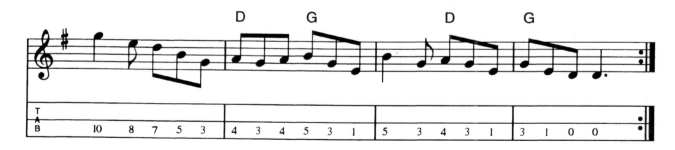

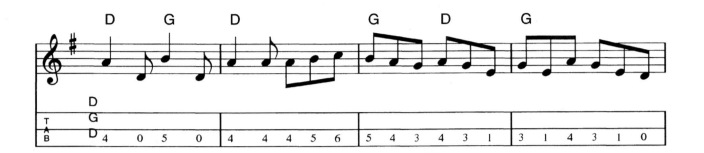

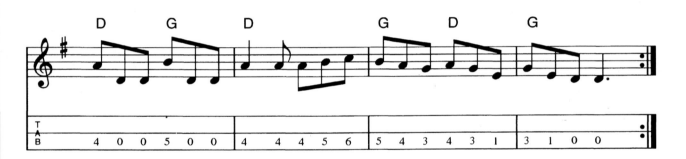

Joe O'Dowd's Jig

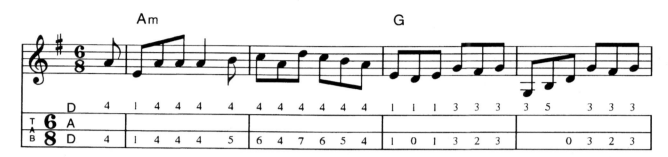

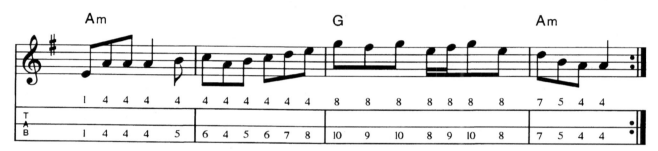

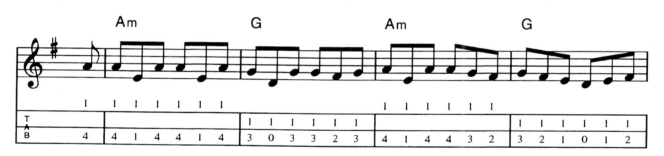

Another Jig Will Do
Slip Jig

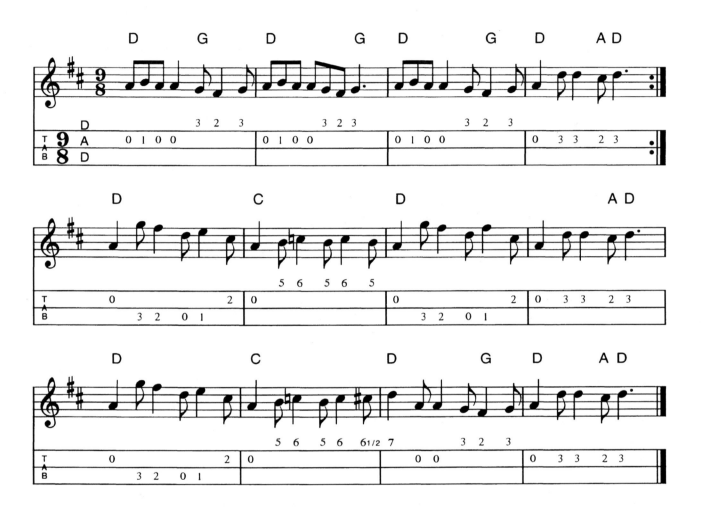

The Drops of Brandy
Slip Jig

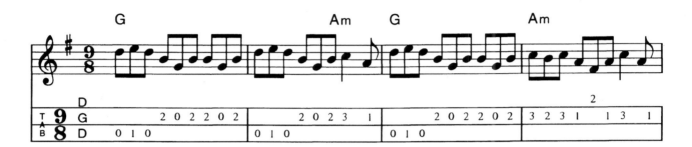

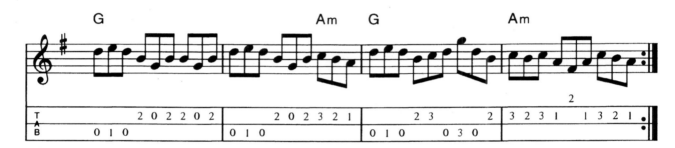

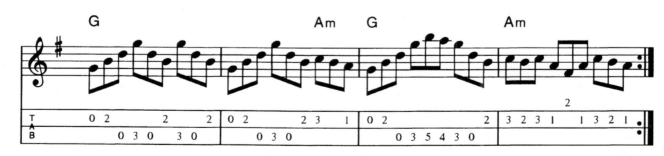

The Boys Of Ballisodare
Slip Jig

The Kid on the Mountain
Slip Jig

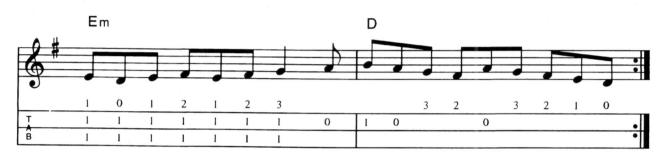

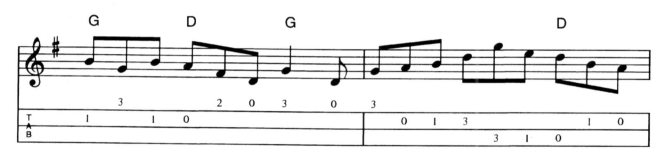

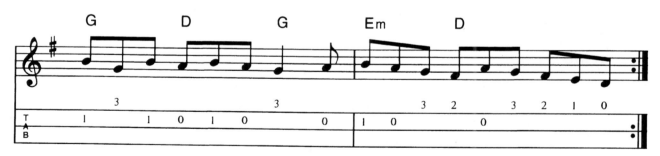

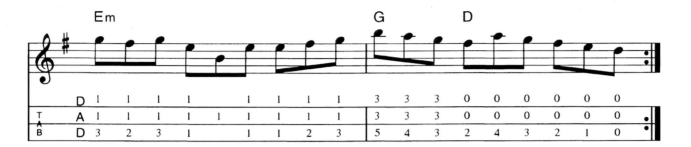

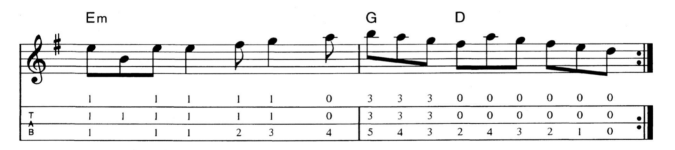

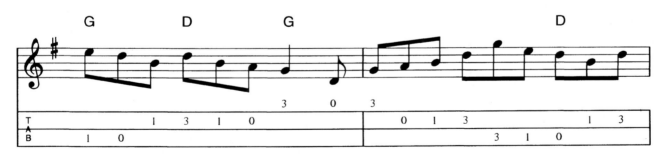

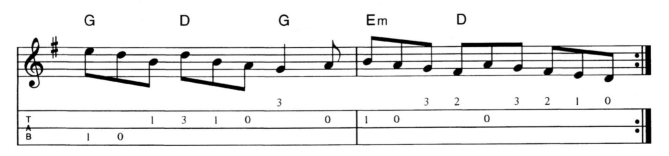

Paddy O'Keefe's Slide

(Dennis Murphy's Slide)

The Star Above the Garter
Slide

Merrily Kissed The Quaker
Slide

The Earl's Chair

Reel

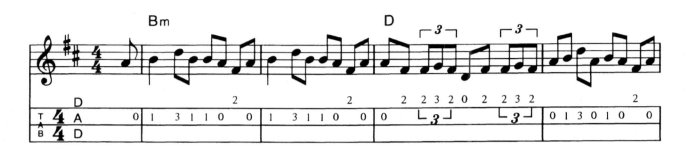

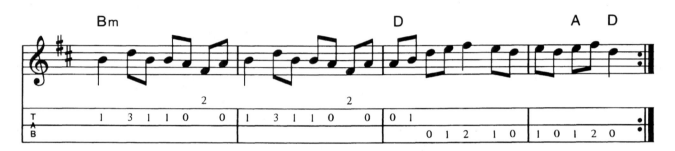

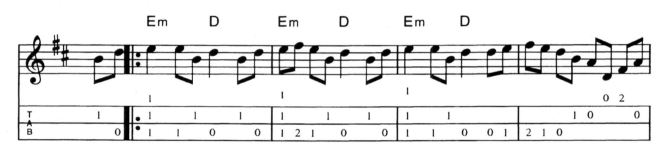

Pigeon on the Gate

Reel

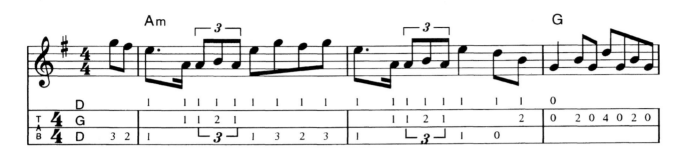

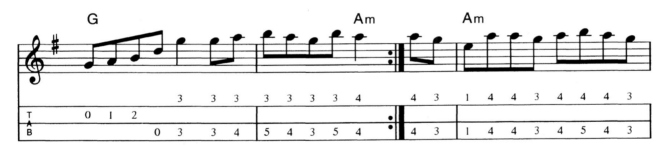

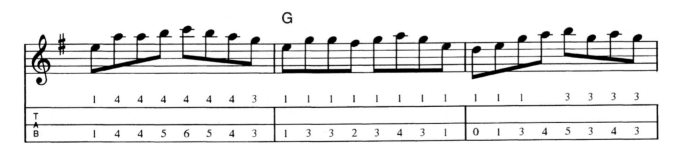

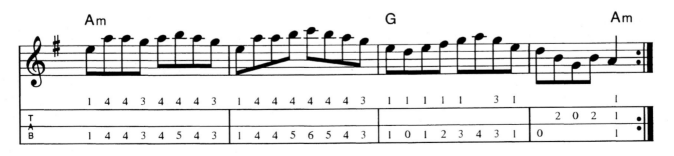

Jenny's Wedding
Reel

The Musical Priest
Reel

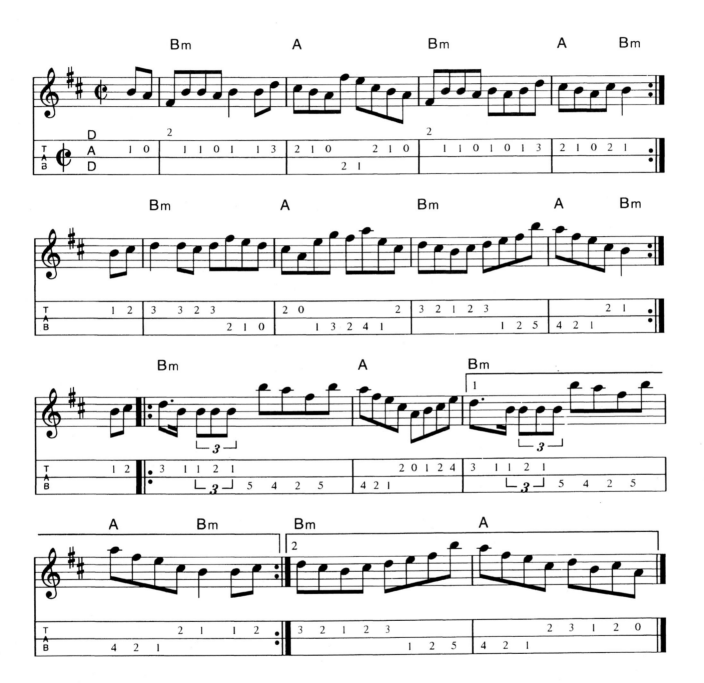

Cooley's Reel

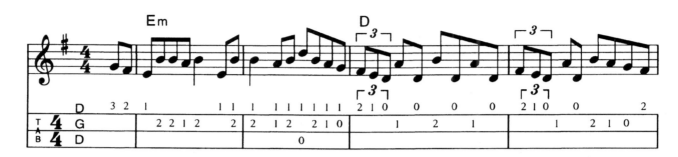

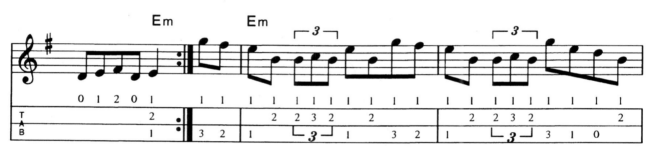

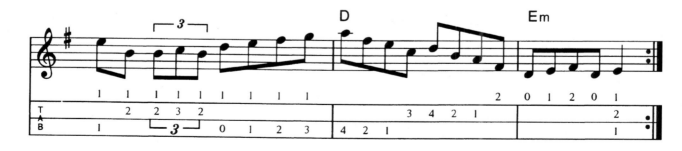

The Ships Are Sailing

Reel

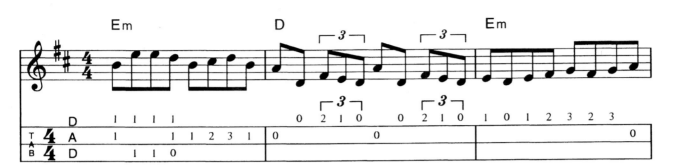

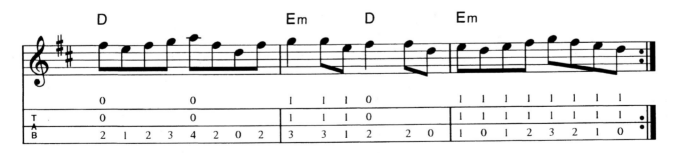

Delahunty's Hornpipe

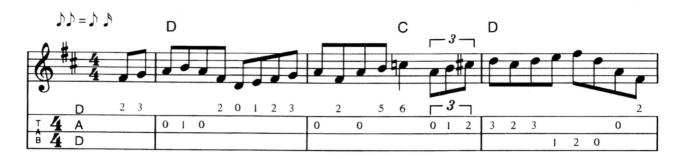

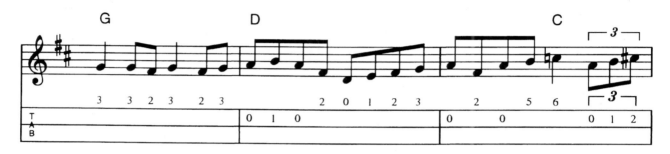

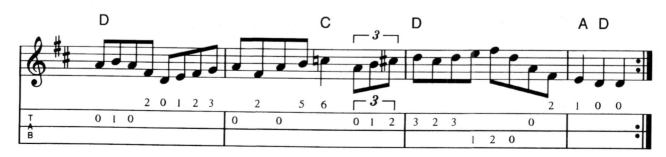

An Comhra Dunn
Hornpipe

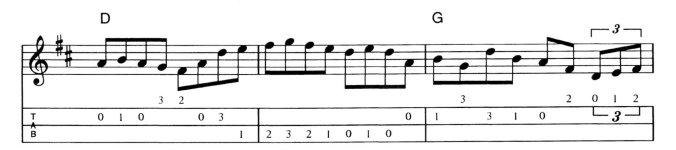

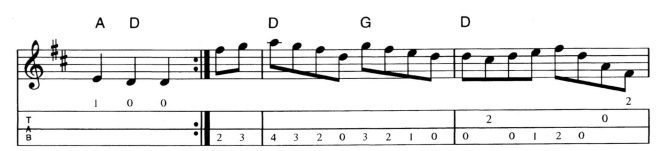

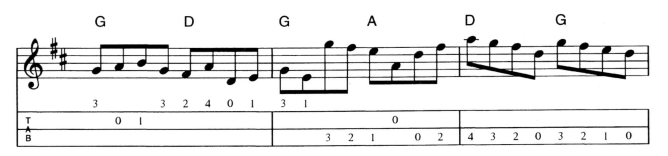

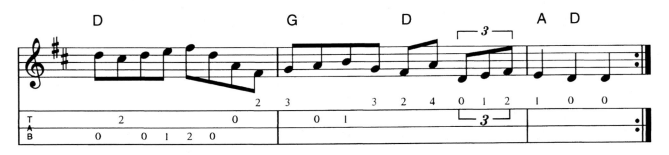

The Rights of Man

Hornpipe

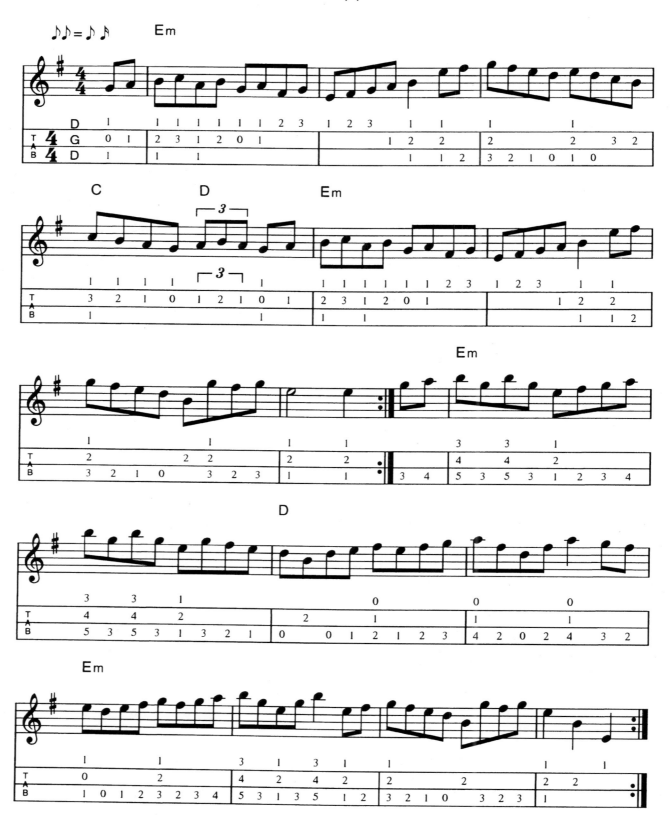

The Rose Tree #1
Polka

The Rose Tree #2

(Port Lairge)
Polka

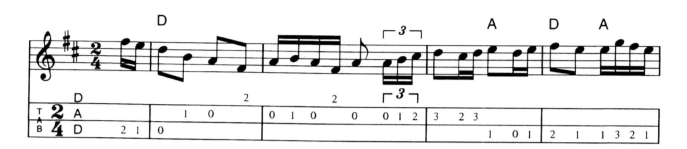

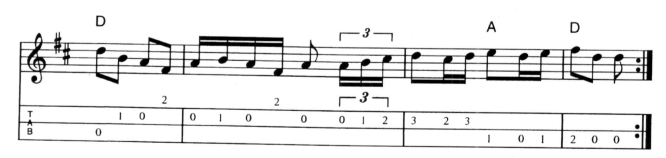

Sonny Brogan's
Mazurka

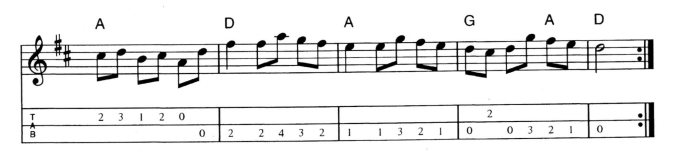

Jackie Donnan's Mazurka

The Downfall of Paris
Set Dance

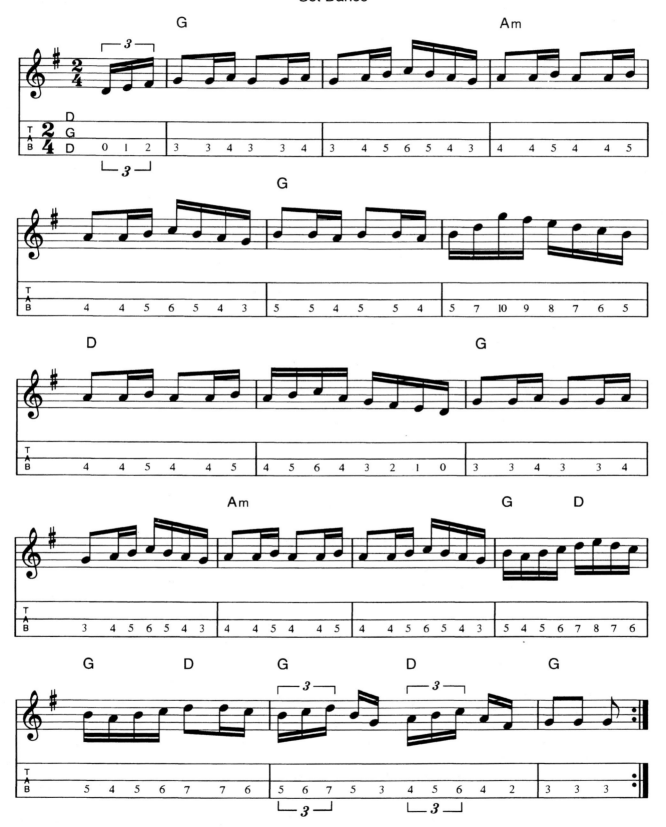

The Lodge Road
Set Dance

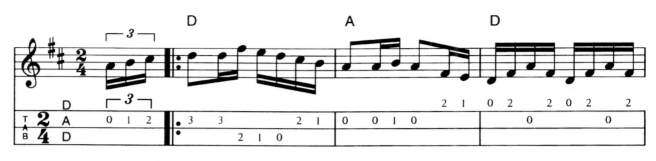

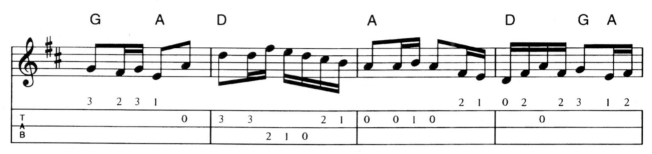

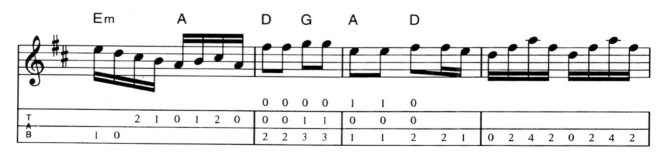

68

Hewlett

Turlough O'Carolan

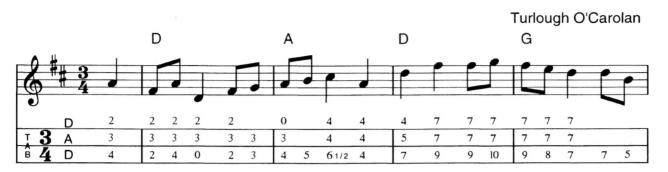

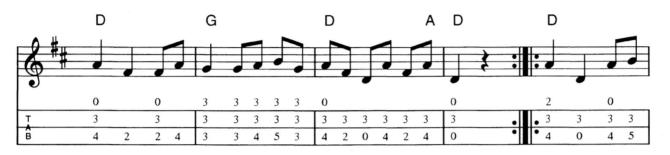

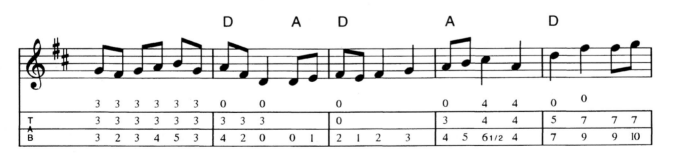

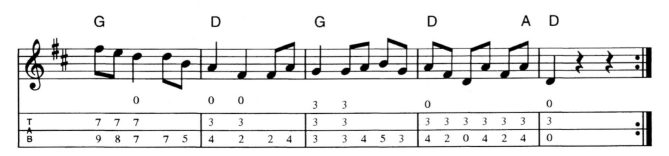

Hugh O'Donnell

Turlough O'Carolan

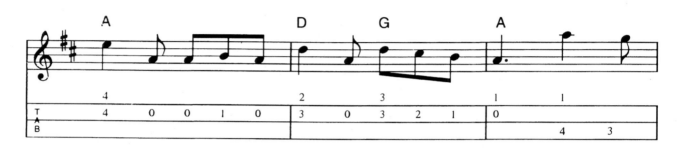

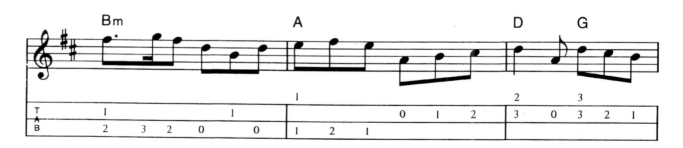

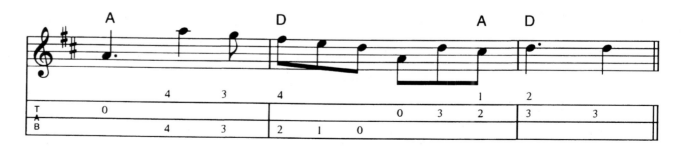

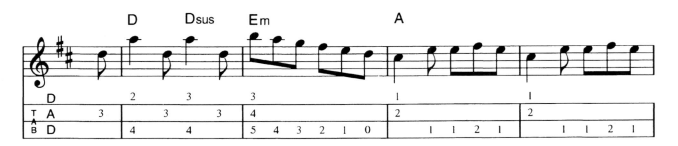

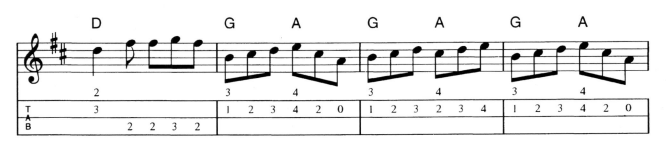

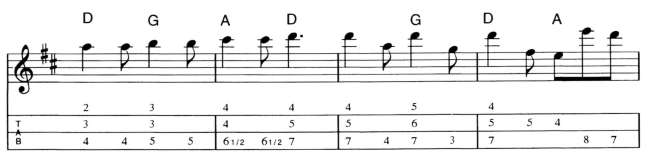

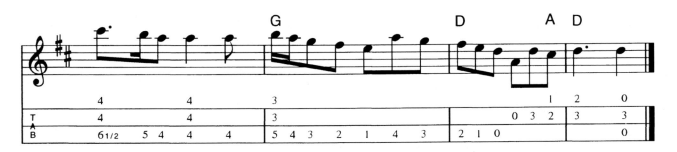

Sí Beg Sí Mor

Turlough O'Carolan

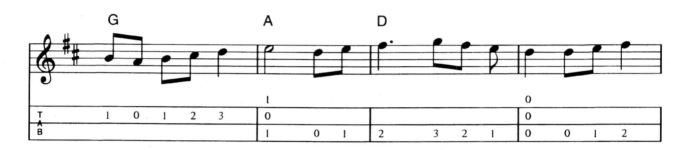

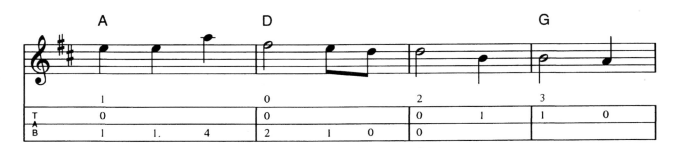

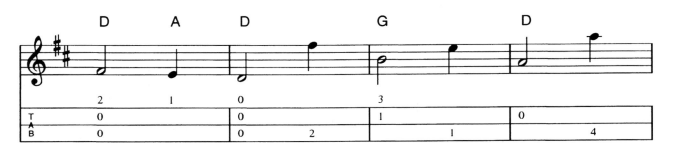

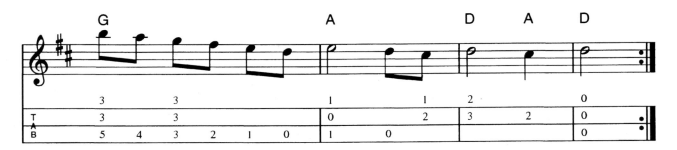

The Clergy's Lamentation

Turlough O'Carolan

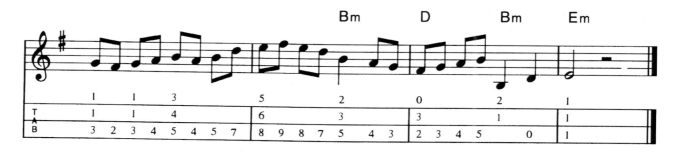

74

The Snowy Breasted Pearl

Turlough O'Carolan

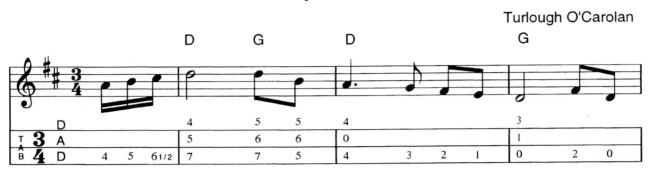

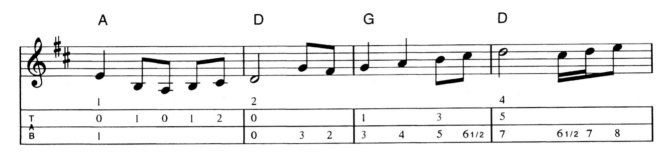

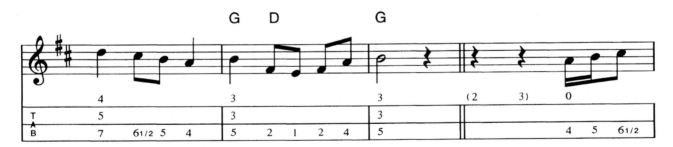

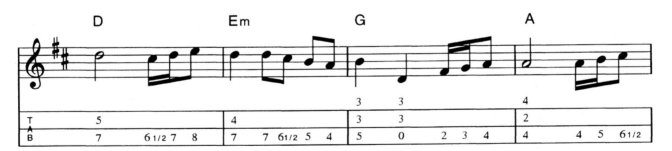

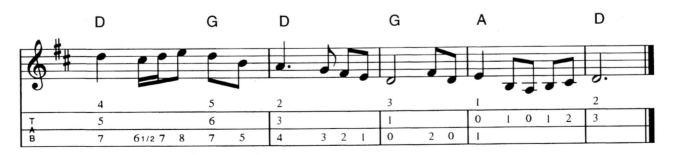

Lord Inchiquin

Turlough O'Carolan

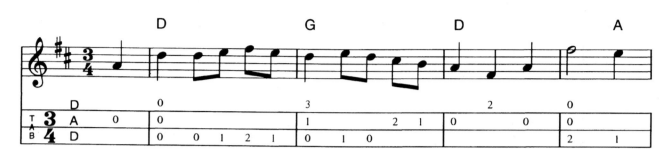

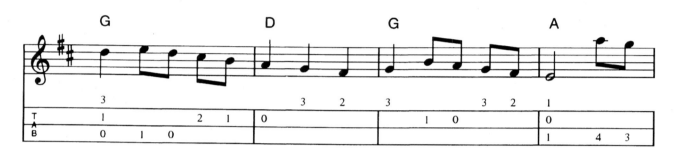

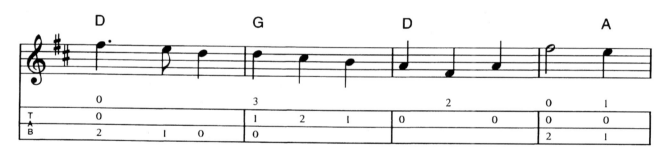

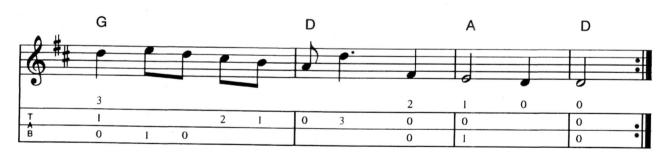

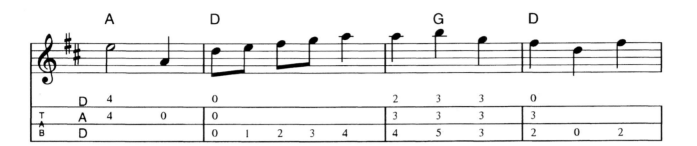

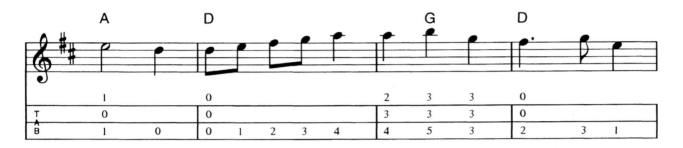

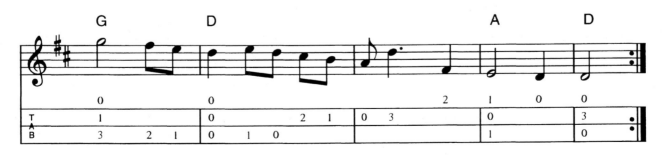

77

O'Carolan's Concerto

Turlough O'Carolan

The Princess Royal

Turlough O'Carolan

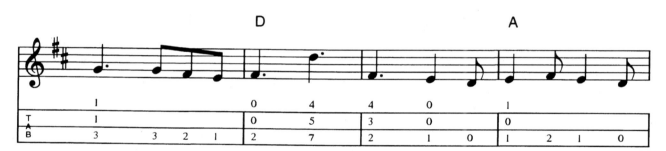

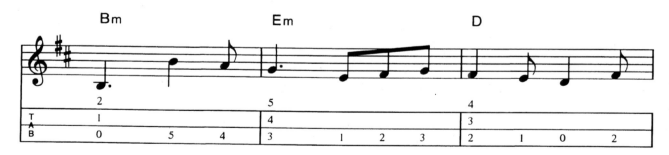

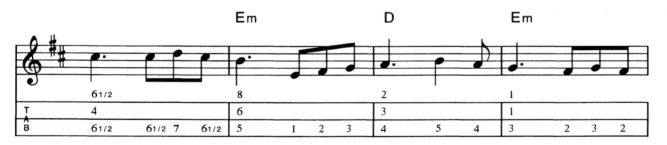

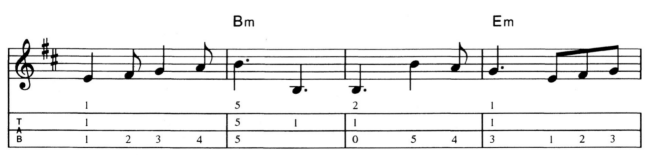

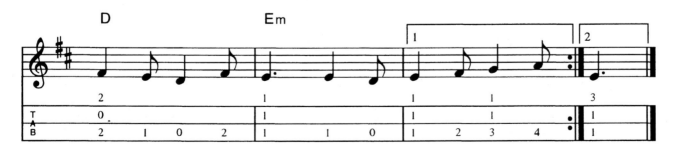

81

Planxty George Brabazon

Turlough O'Carolan

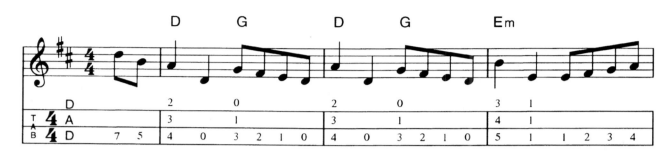

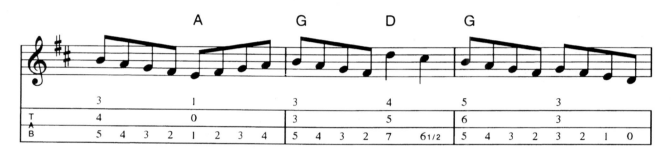

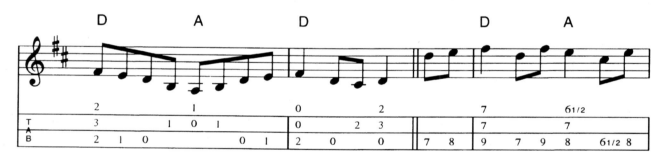

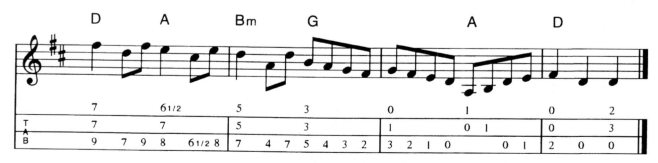

Airde Chuain

The Quiet Land of Erin

Air

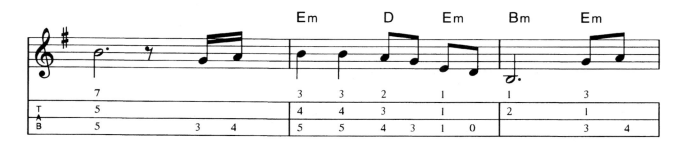

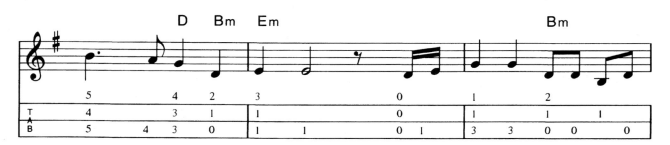

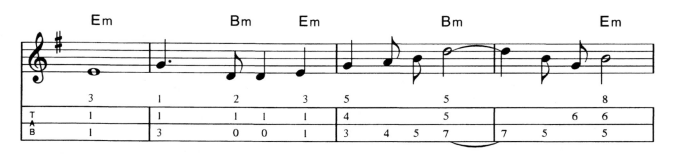

Sí Bhean Locha Léin

Air

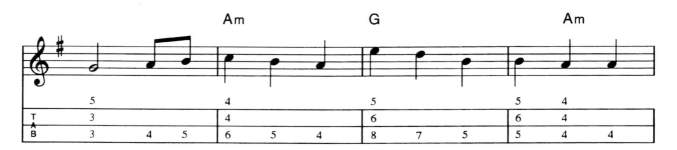

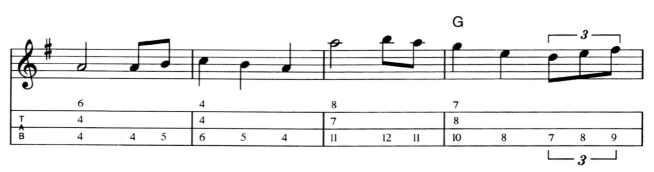

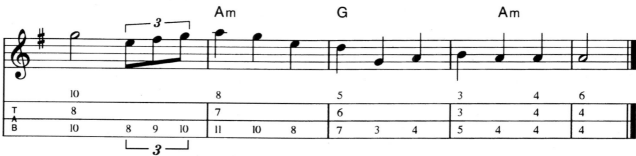

Cailm Son

The Brown Maid
Slow Air

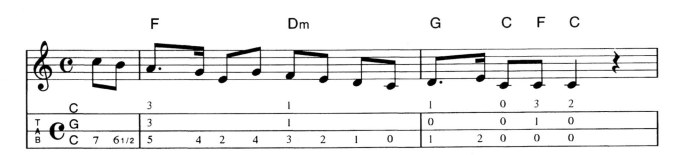

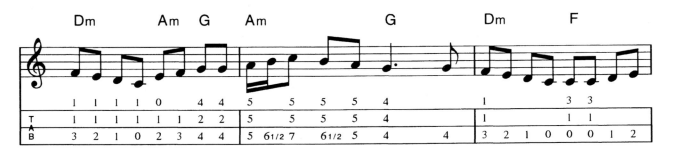

Eamonn an Chnoic

Edmund Ryan

Air

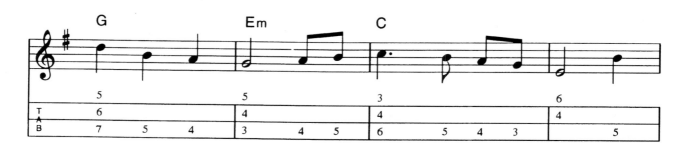

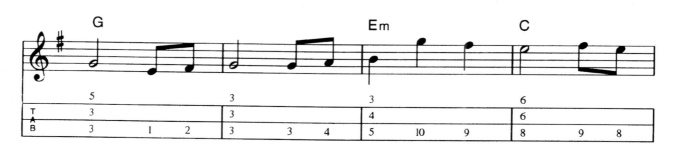

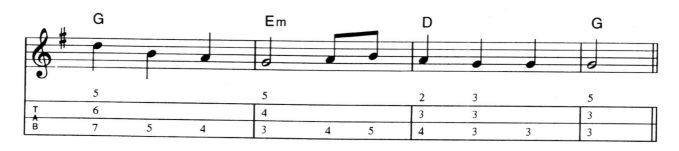

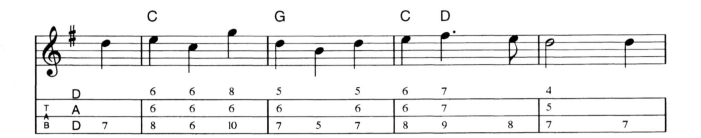

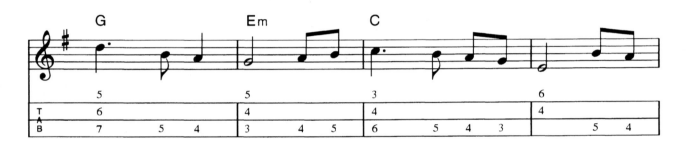

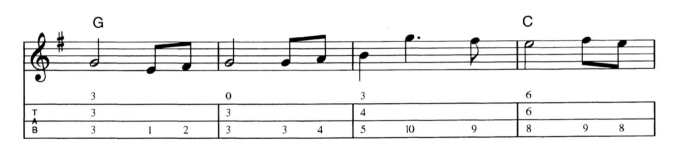

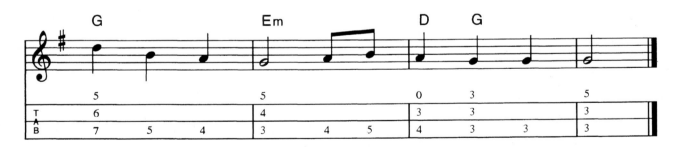

Give Me Your Hand

Rory Dall O' Cathain

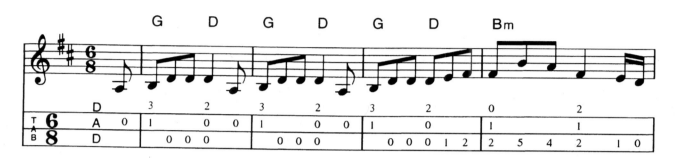

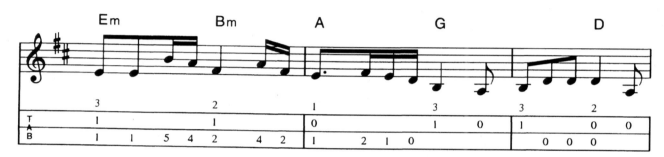

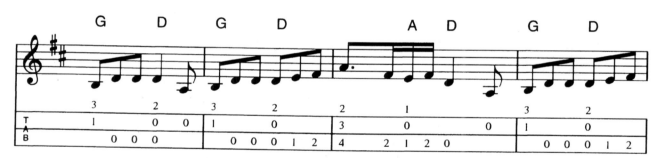

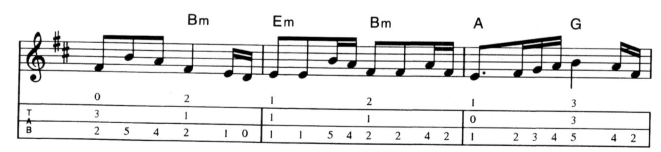

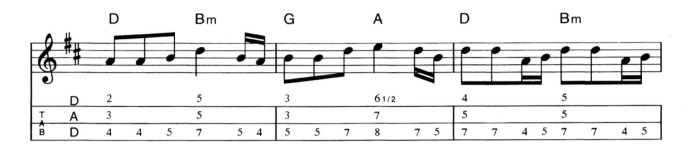

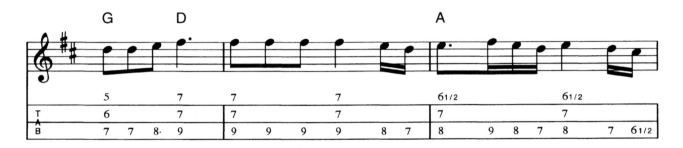

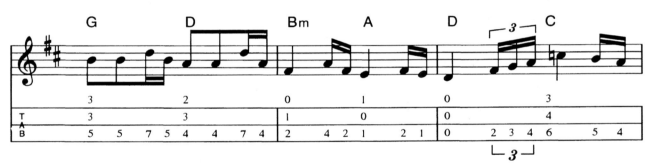

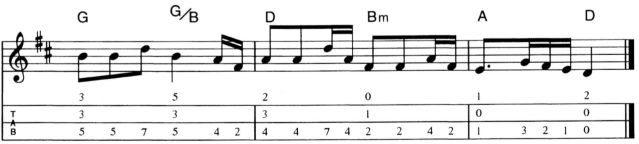

90

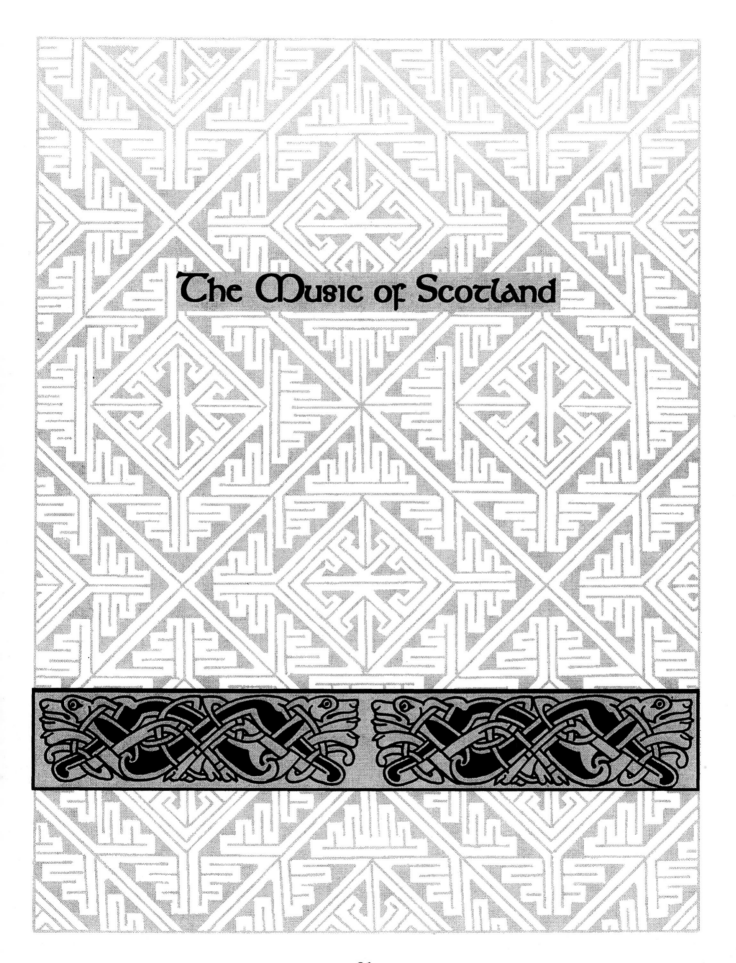

The Music of Scotland

Campbell's Farewell to Red Castle

(Campbell's Farewell to Redgap)

March

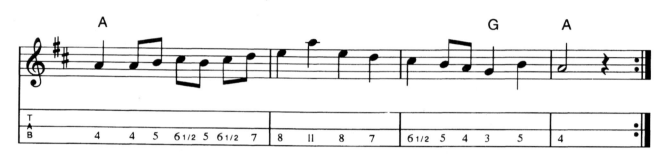

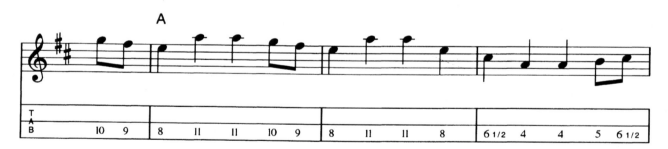

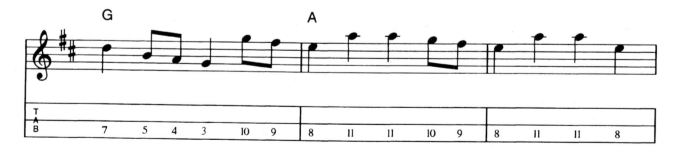

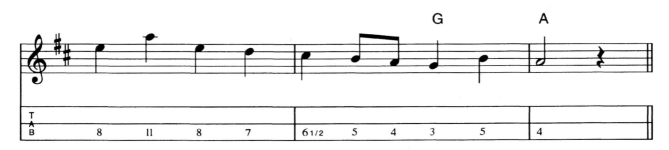

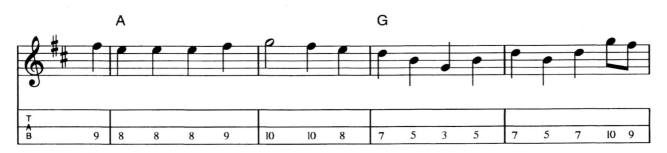

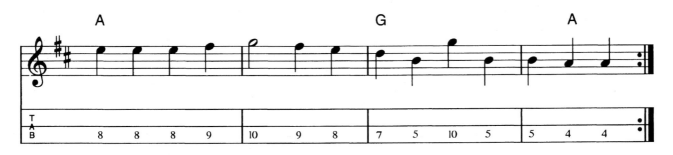

Piobaireachd of Donald Ohu

March

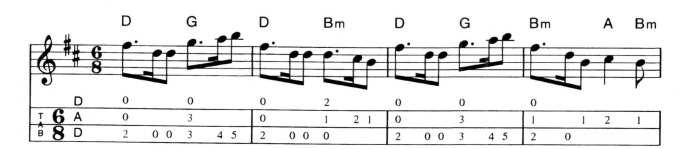

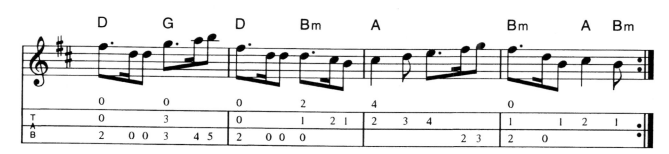

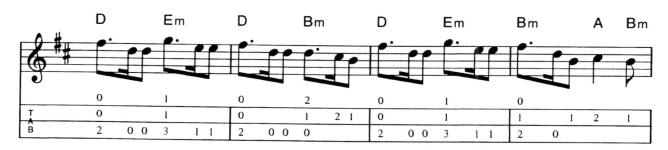

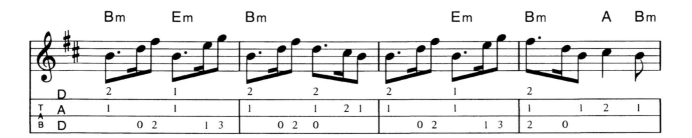

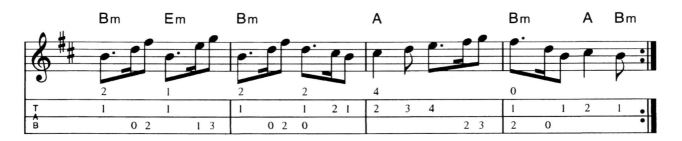

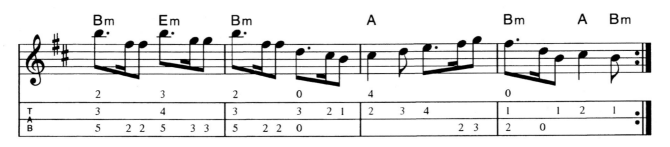

Scotland the Brave

March

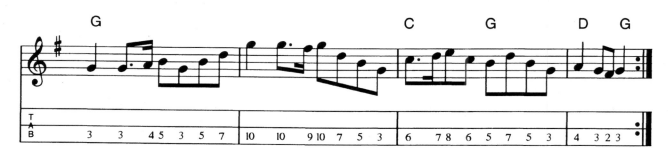

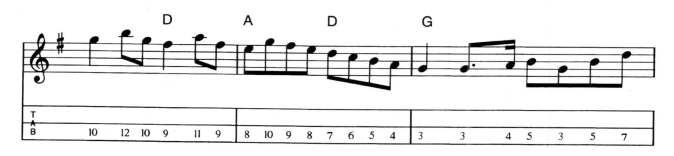

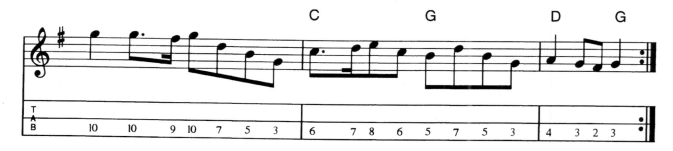

Kilcoy's March

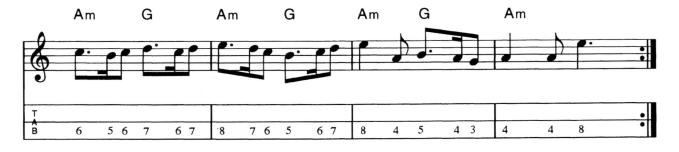

The Duke of Fife
March

98

The Cameron Highlanders

March

J. Scott Skinner

99

Miss Drummond of Perth

Strathspey

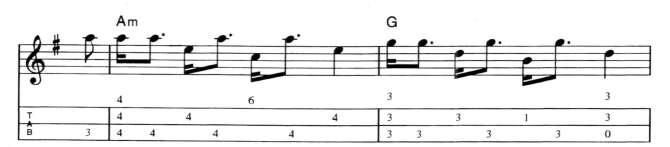

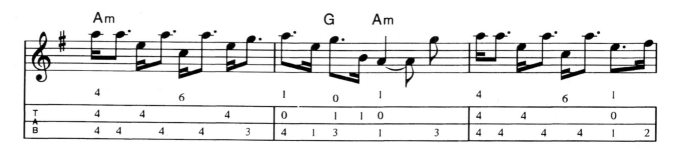

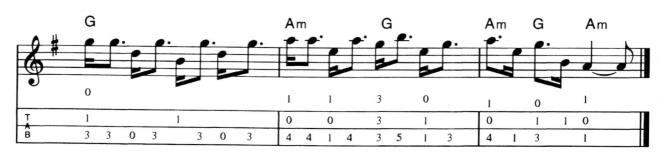

The Duchess of Athole's Slipper
Strathspey

Niel Gow

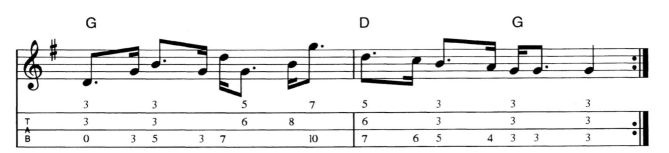

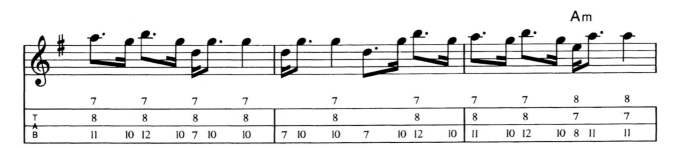

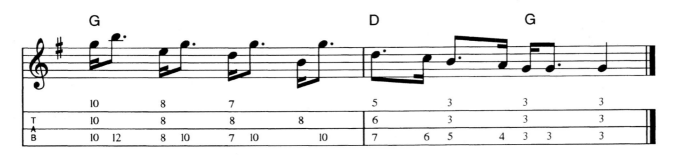

Highland Whiskey

Strathspey

Niel Gow

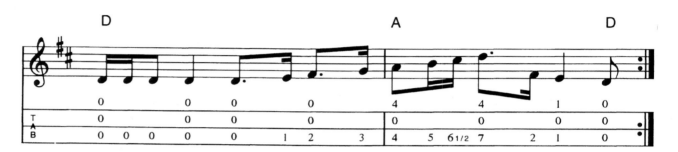

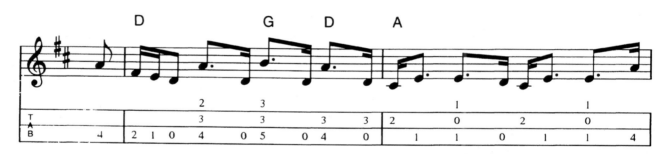

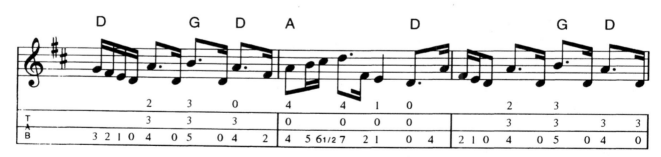

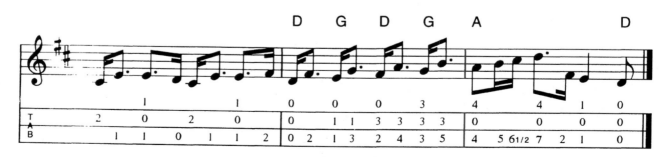

102

Mairi's Wedding
Country Dance

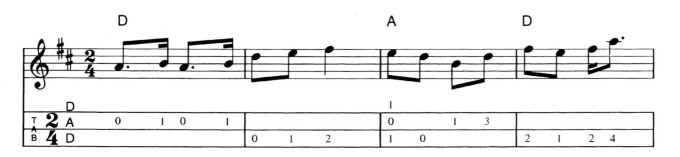

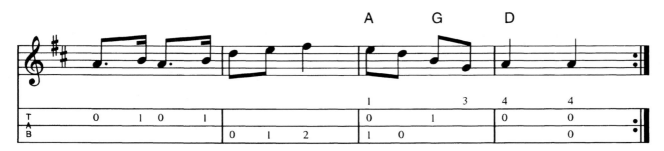

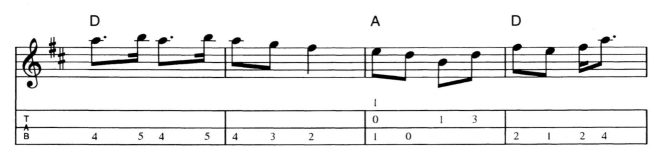

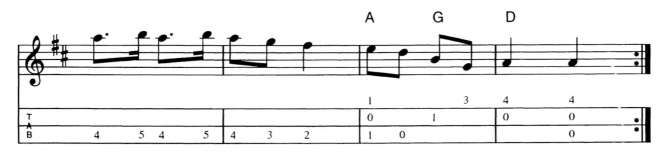

Harvest Home
Hornpipe

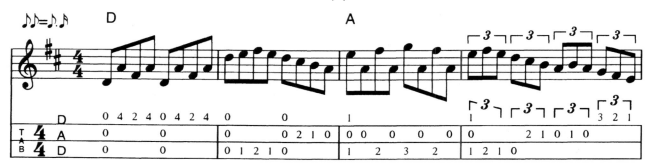

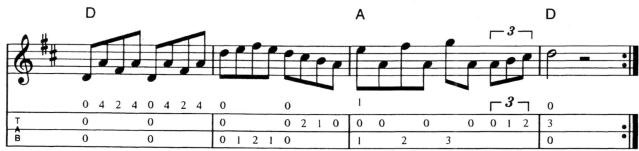

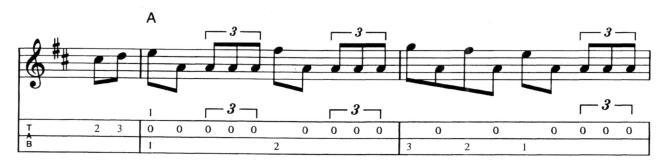

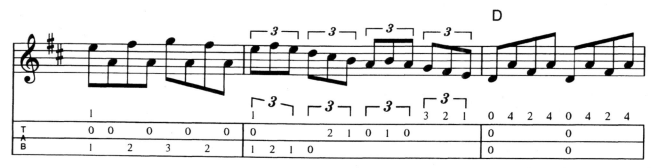

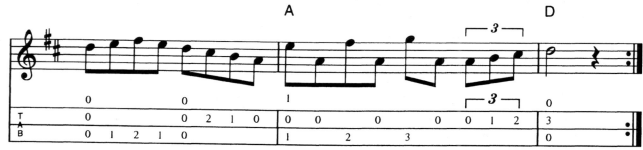

Staten Island
Hornpipe

Morpath Rant

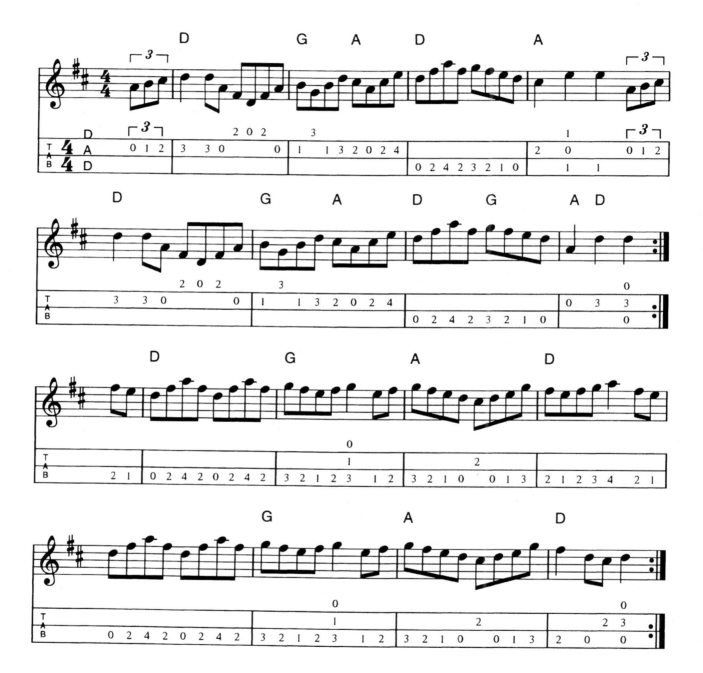

Petronella
Country Dance

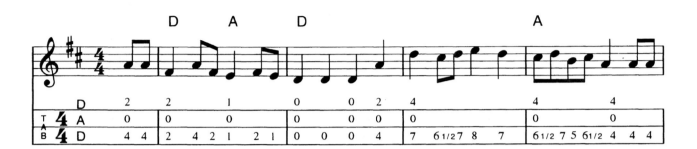

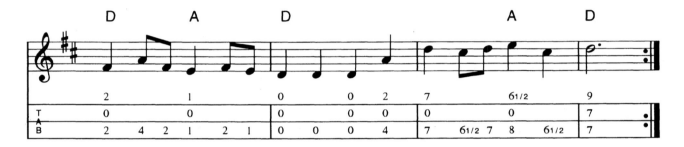

Dulcimer sounds one octave lower than written for B section:

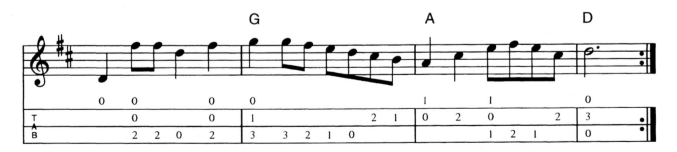

107

The White Cockade

Reel

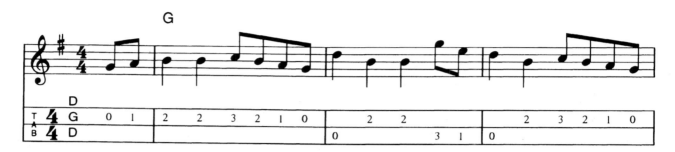

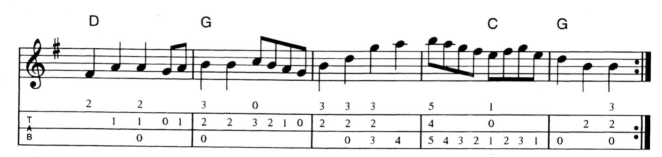

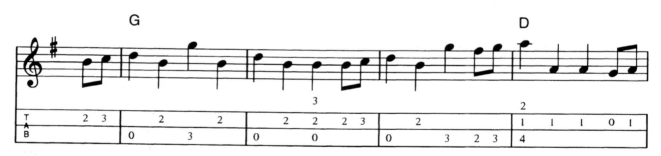

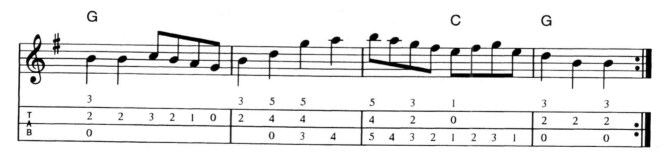

Miss McCleod's Reel

109

The Flowers of Edinburgh
Reel

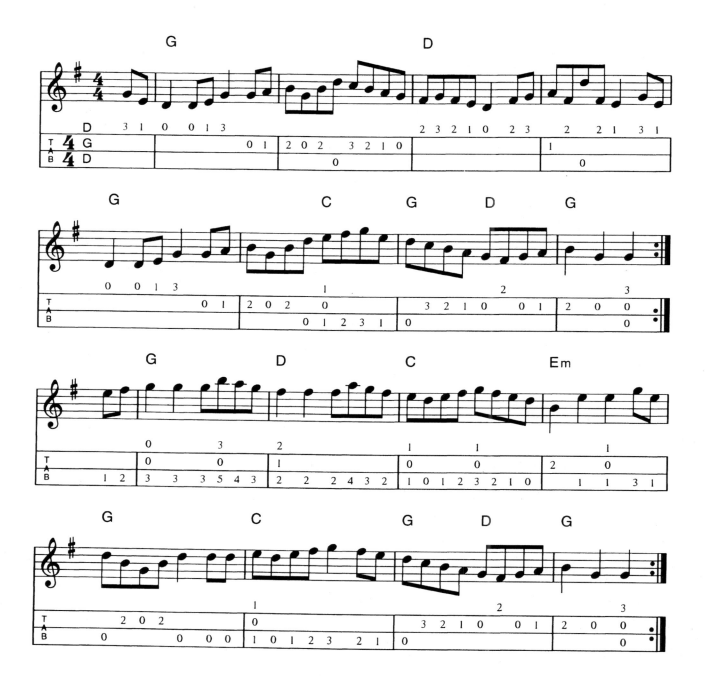

The Soldier's Joy
Reel

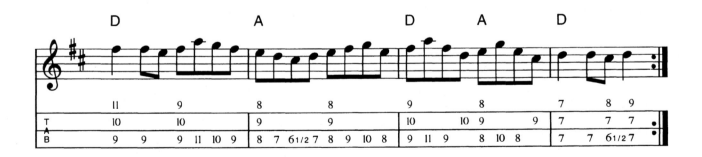

Jack Broke da Prison Door

Shetland Reel

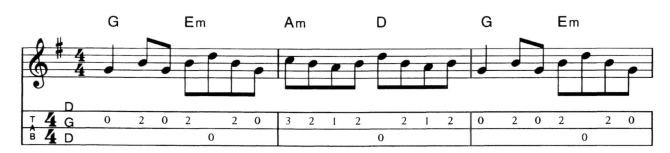

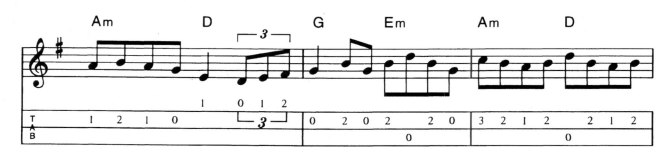

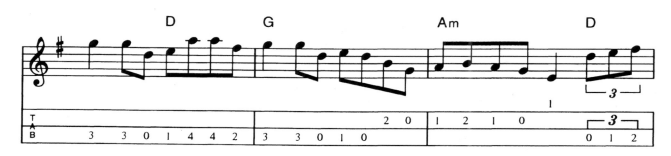

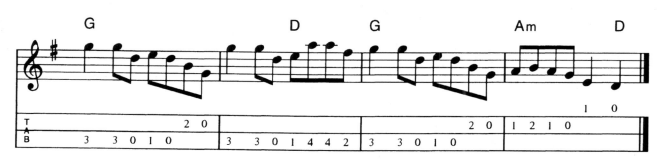

Far From Home
Shetland Island Reel

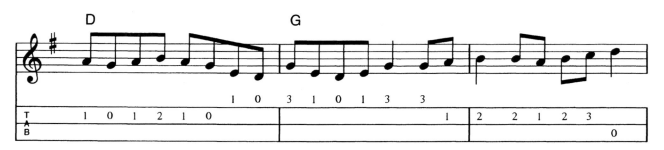

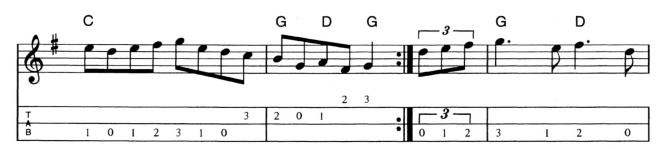

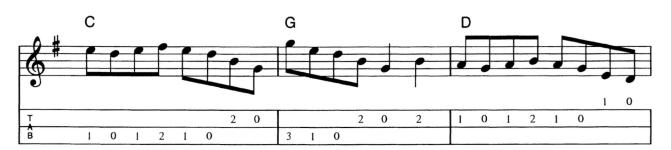

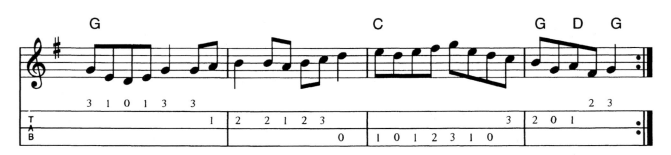

Christmas Day Ida Moarnin'
Shetland Islands

The Aith Rant
Shetland Trowie Tune

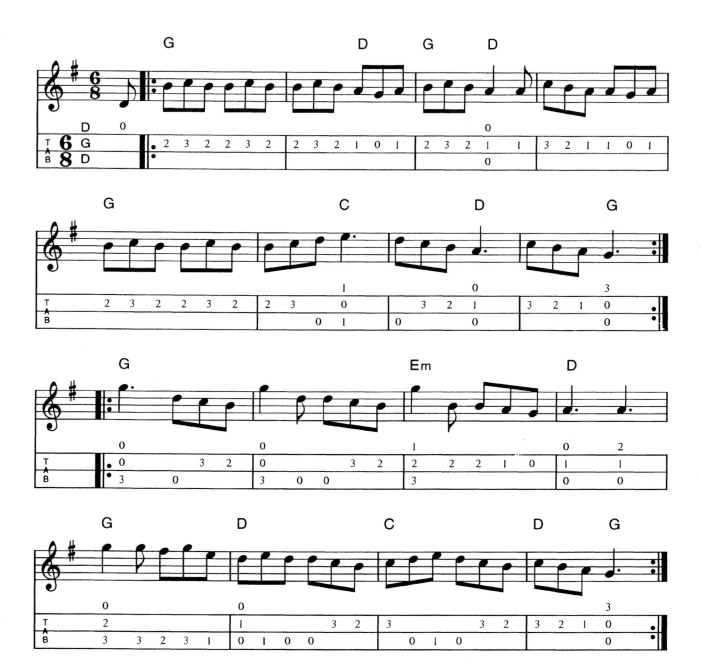

The Bonnie Lass of Bon Accord

J. Scott Skinner

Oran Mór MacLeód
The MacCleod's Big Tune

Rory Dall Morrison

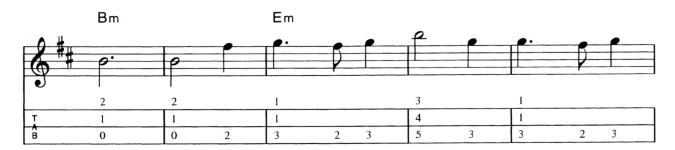

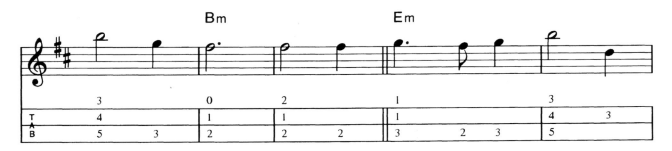

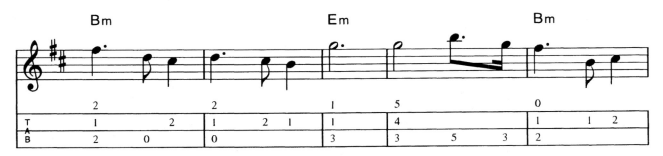

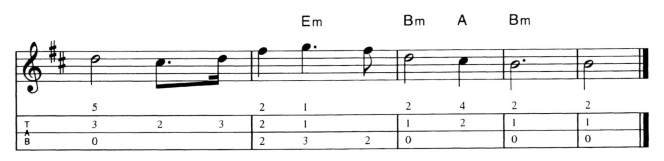

Mairi Mhin Meall-Shuileach
Waltz

Fingerpicked

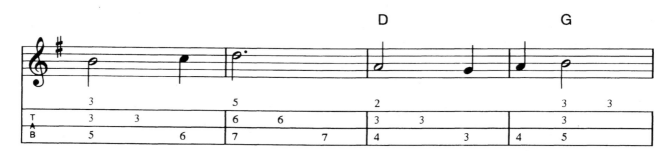

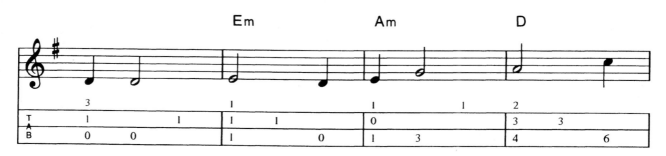

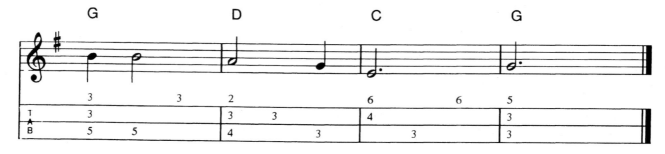

Farewell To Whiskey

Lament

Niel Gow

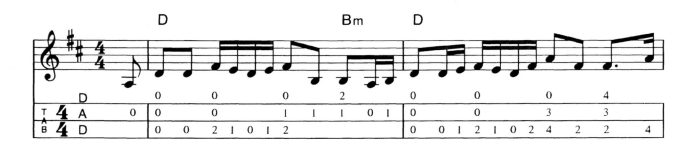

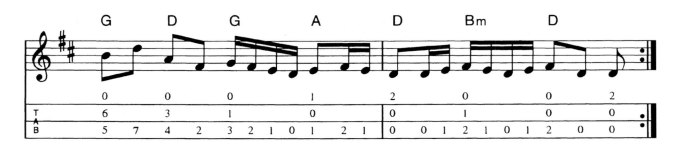

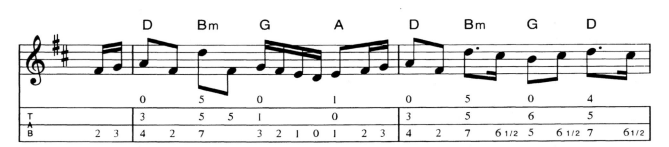

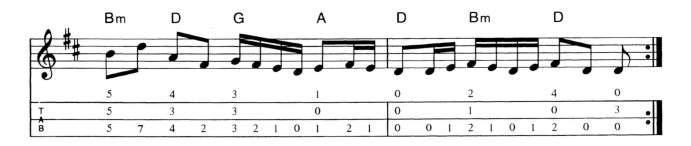

The Skye Boat Song

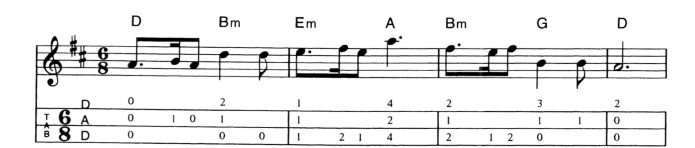

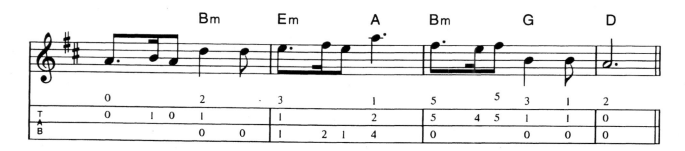

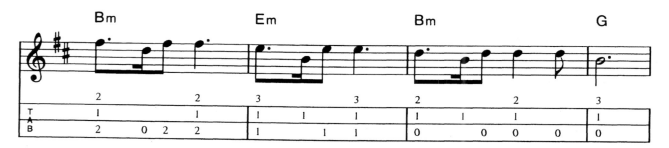

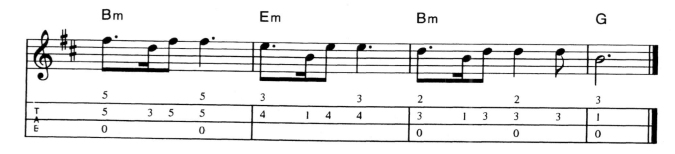

Princess Augusta

Niel Gow

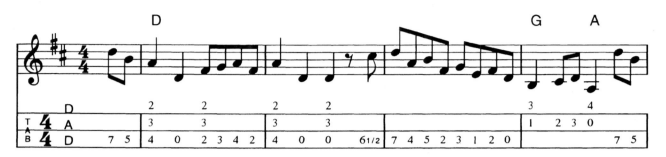

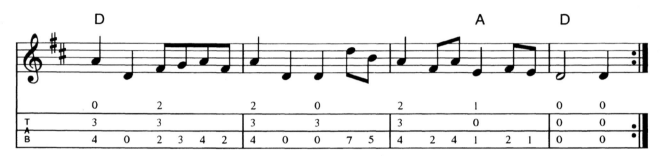

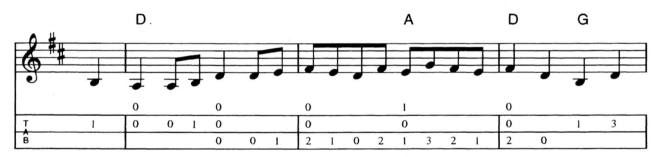

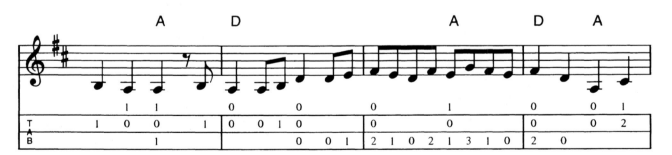

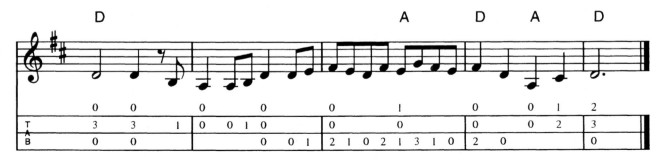

My Home
Waltz

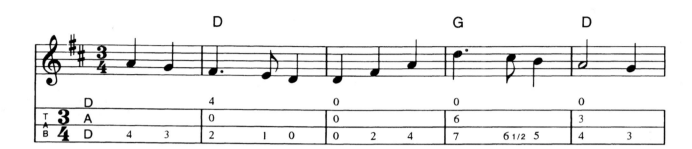

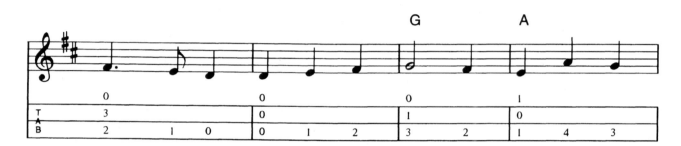

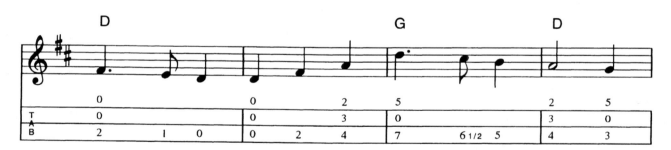

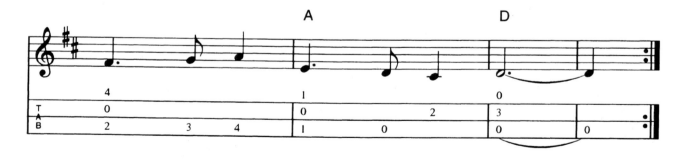

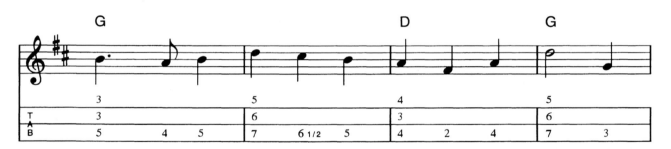

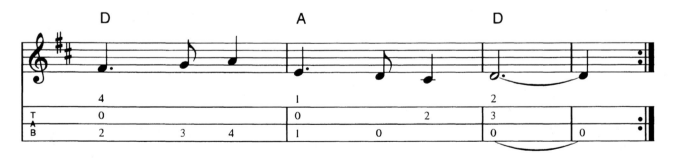

Crodh Chinn Taile

The Cattle of Kintail
Slow Air

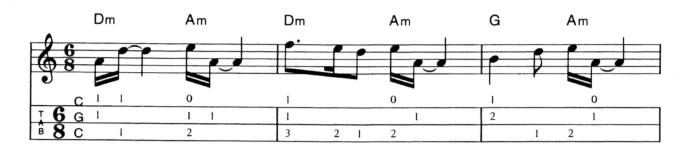

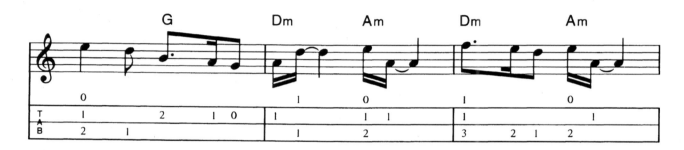

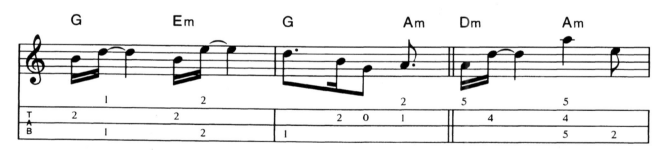

Loch Lomond
Song

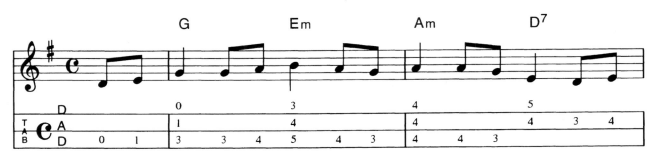

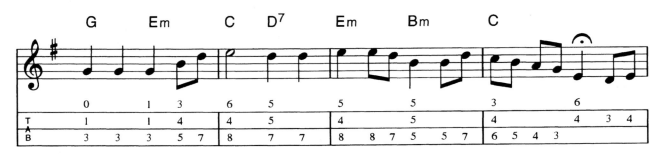

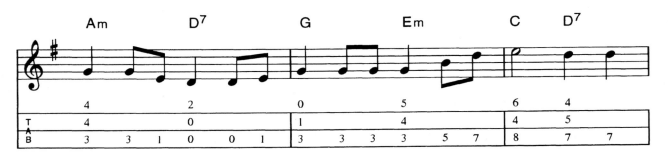

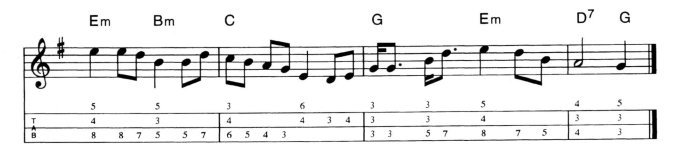

The Trip We Took Over the Mountain
Waltz

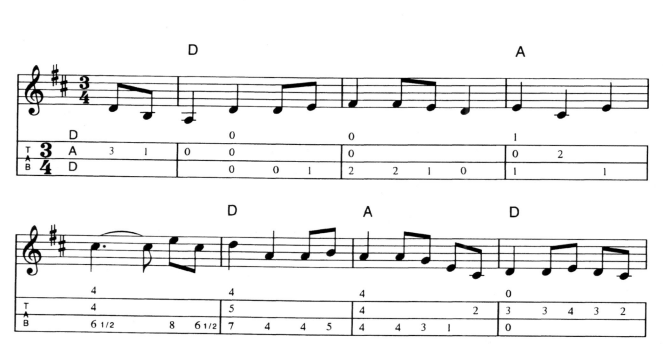

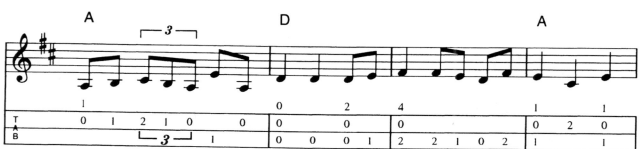

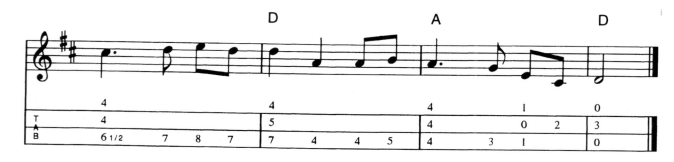

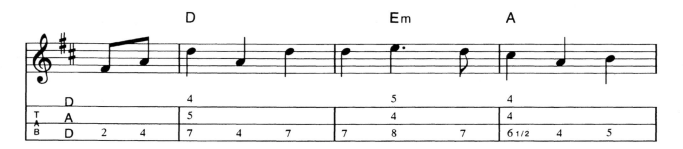

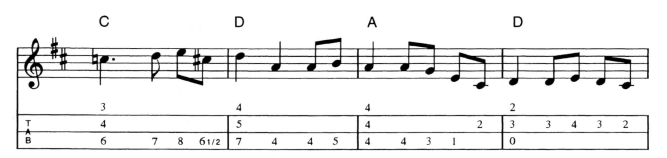

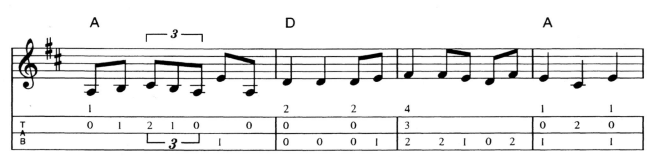

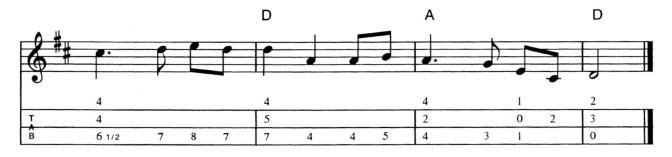

The Arran Boat
Slow Air

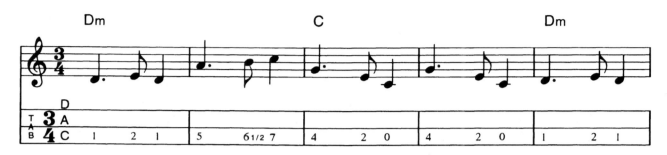

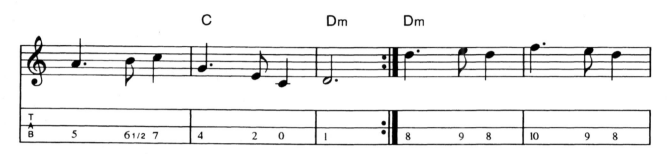

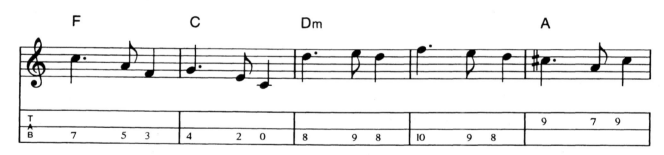

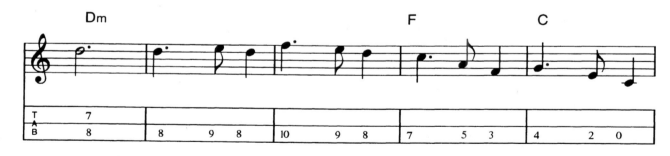

I Was Roaming in the Gloaming
Air

The Cruiskin
Air

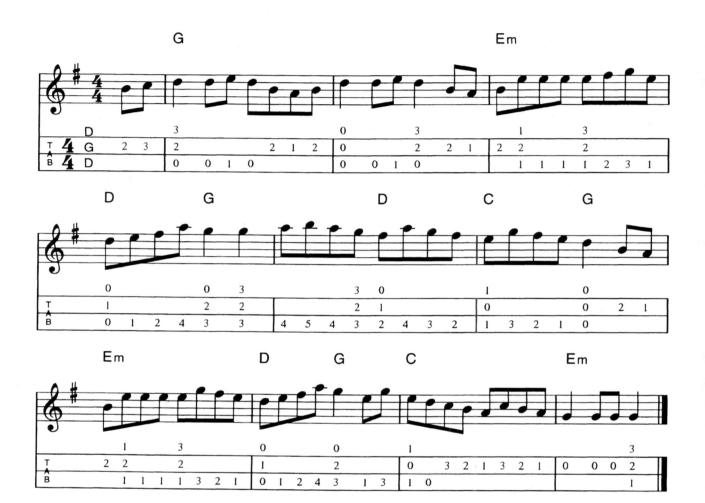

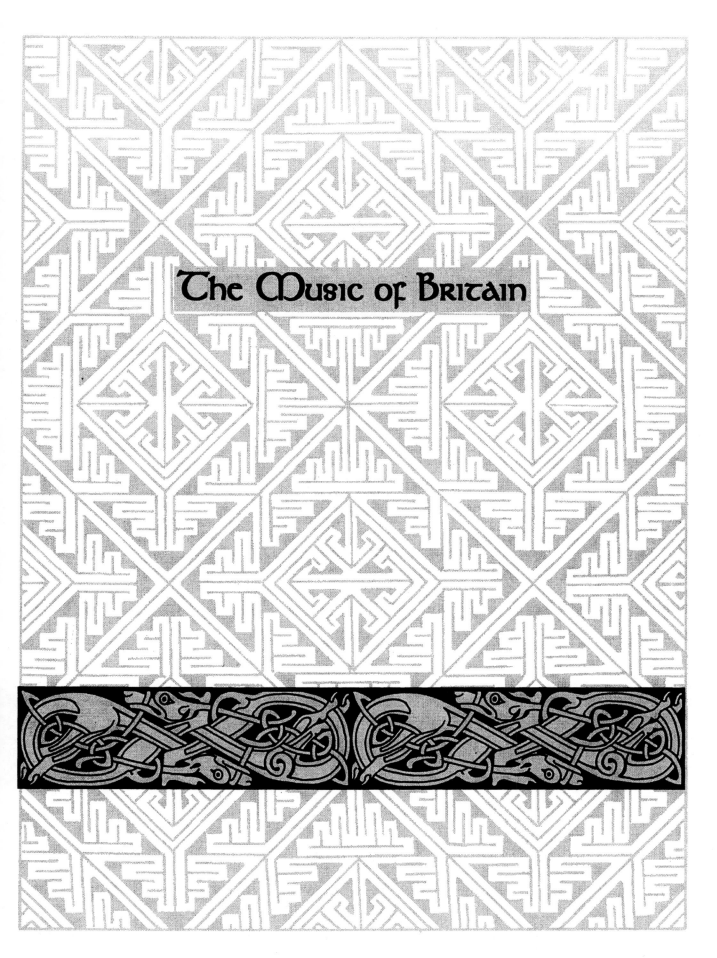

The Music of Britain

Trunkles

Oddington Morris

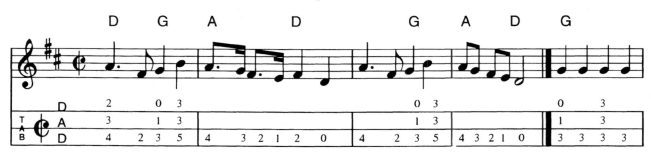

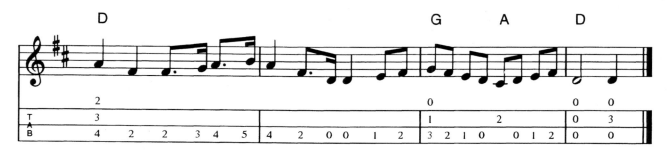

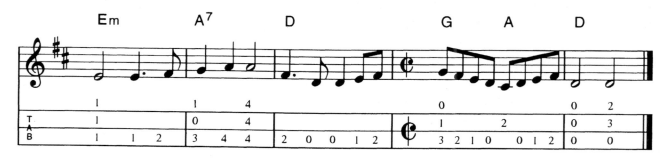

Dance to Your Daddy

Country Dance, Northumberland

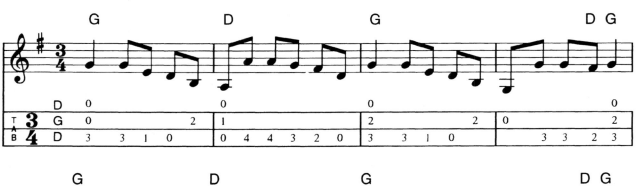

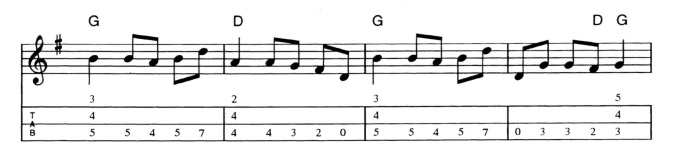

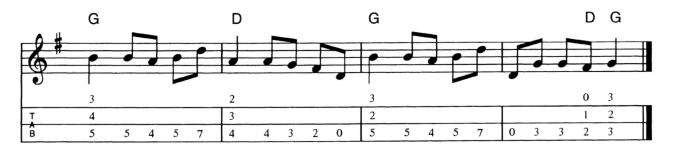

Princess Royal

Ducklington Morris Dance

(from O'Carolan)

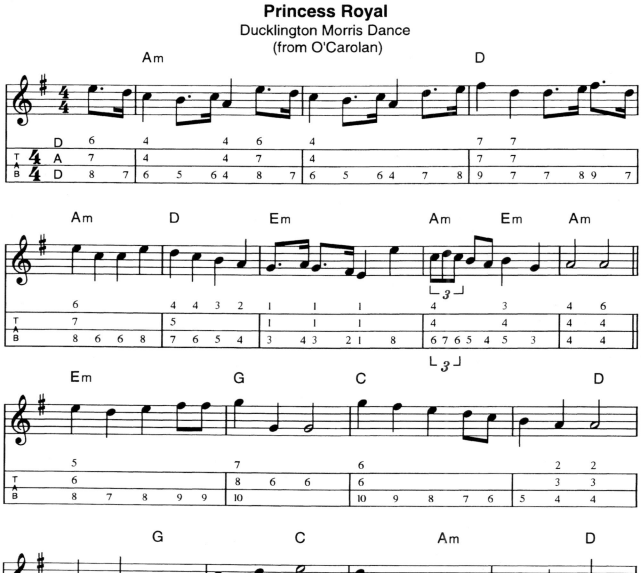

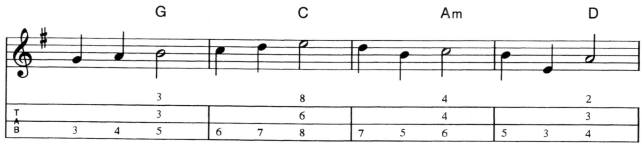

The Old Frog Dance
Oddington Hanky Dance

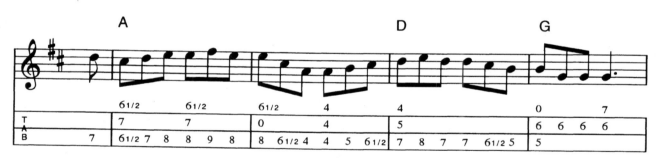

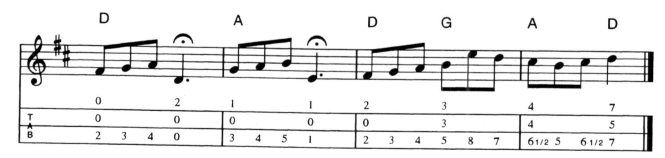

Idbury Hill
Morris Dance

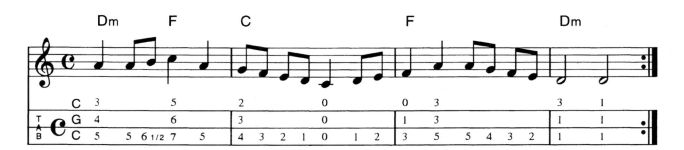

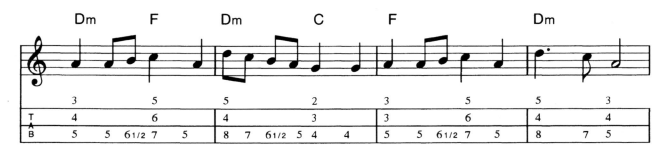

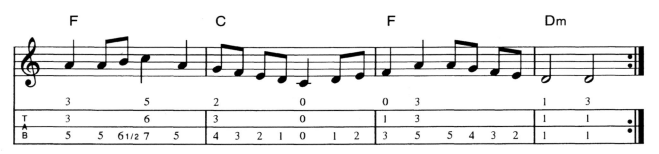

Can Cala Me

May Day Song from Padstow, Cornwall

138

The Cuckoo's Nest
County Dance

Child Grove

Country Dance

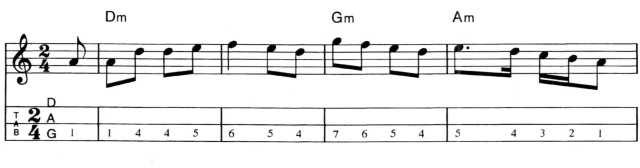

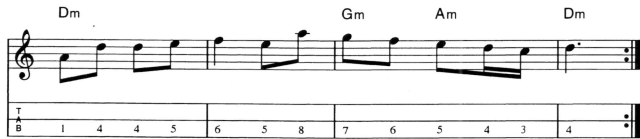

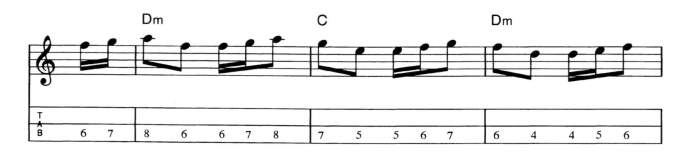

The Ashgrove
Song

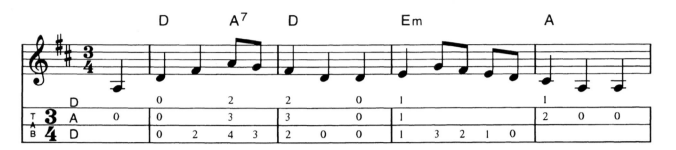

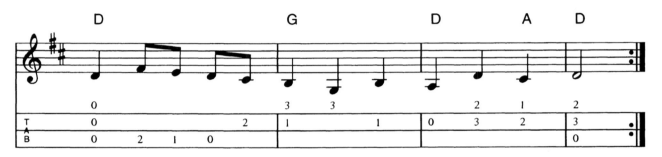

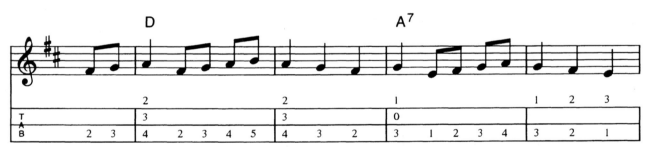

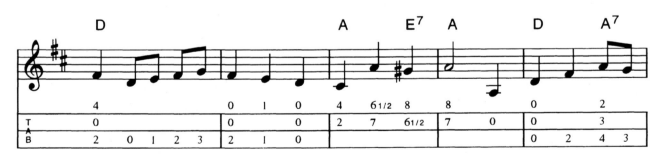

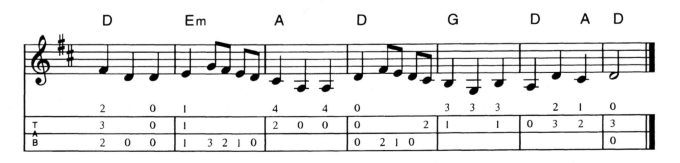

All Through the Night

Ar Hyd y Nos

Lullaby

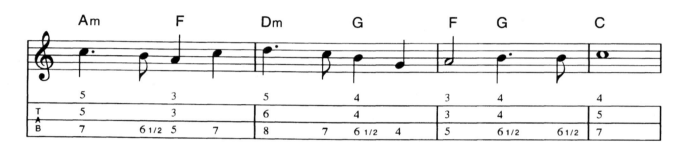

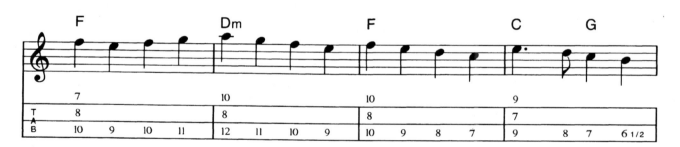

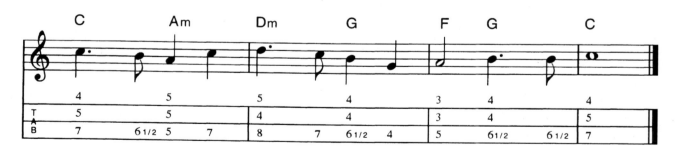

Morfa Rhuddlan

The Marsh of Rhuddlan

Lament

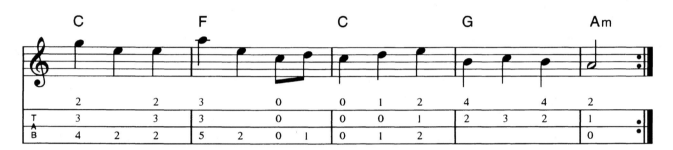

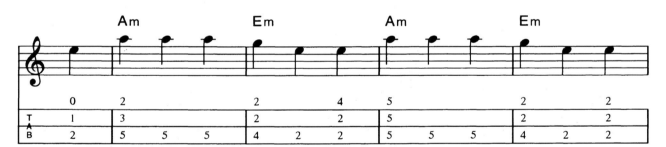

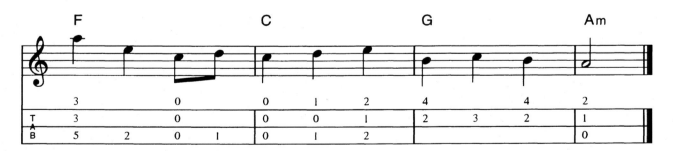

Ffarweliwch, Rwy'n Madal A'm Gwlad

Farewell, For I am Leaving My Land

Air

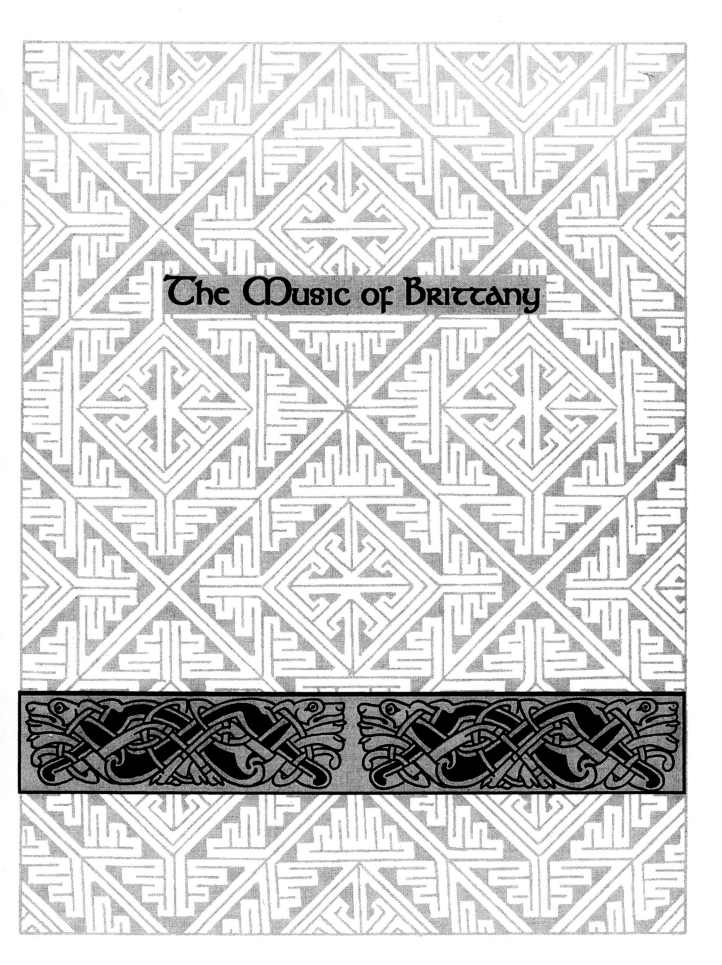

The Music of Brittany

Dans Mod Koh a Vaod
Dance Suite

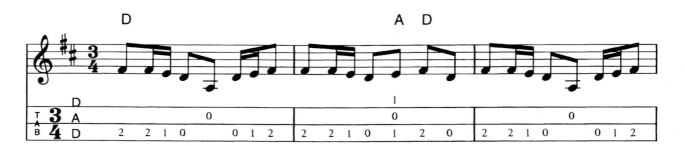

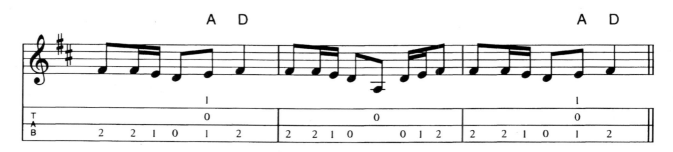

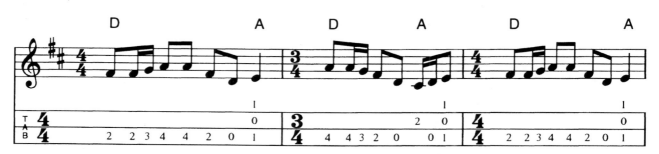

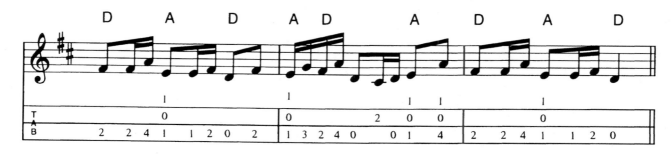

147

Peh Trouz 'Zou ar en Doar

What Noise on Earth?
Christmas Carol

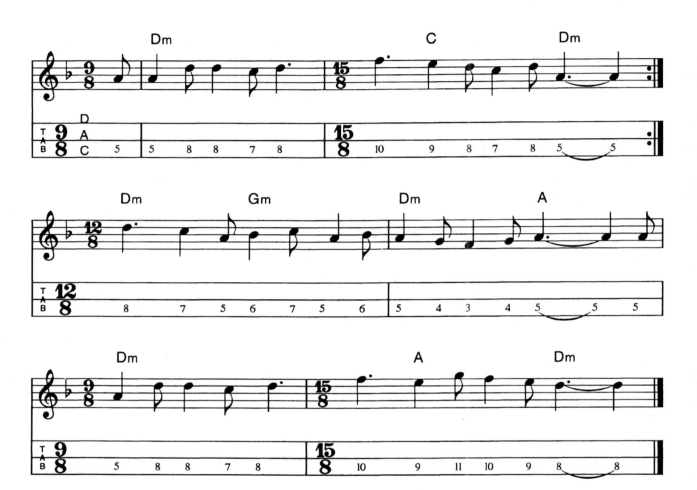

Wedding Tune

March from Leuelan

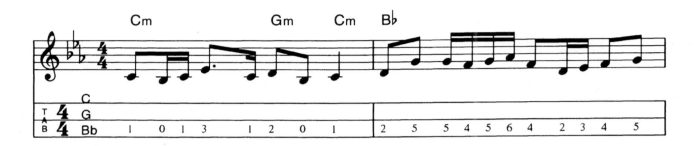

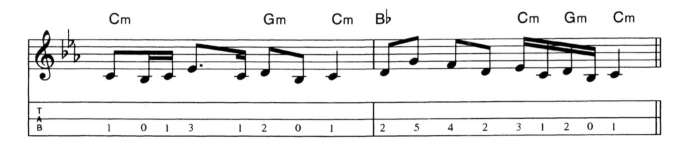

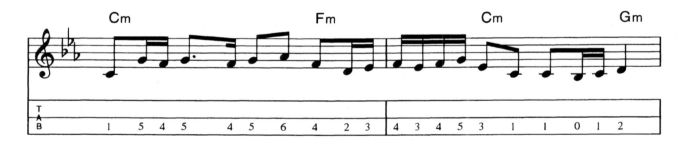

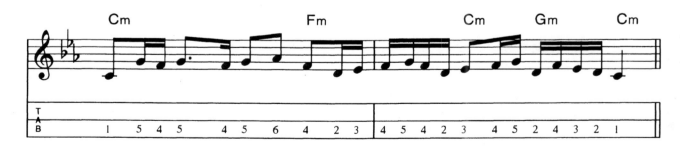

150

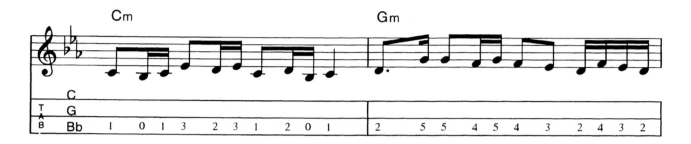

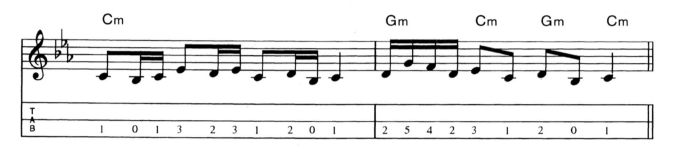

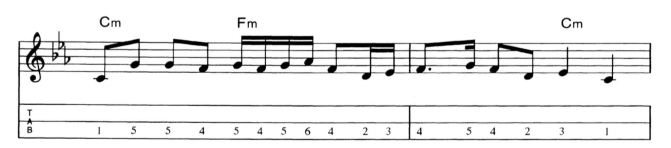

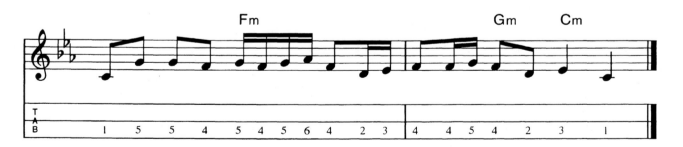

An Dro
from Noalou

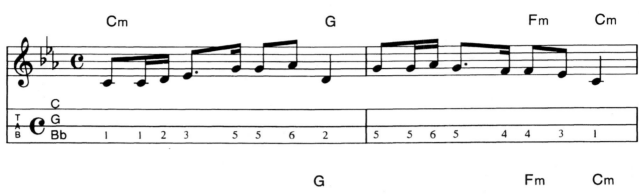

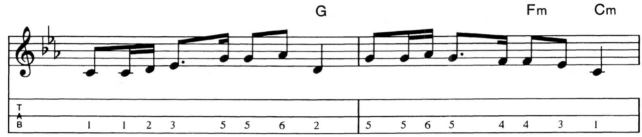

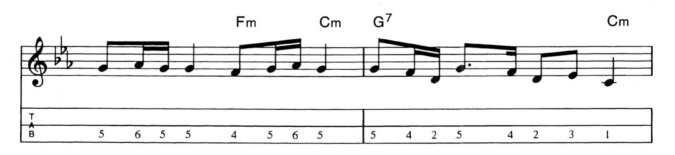

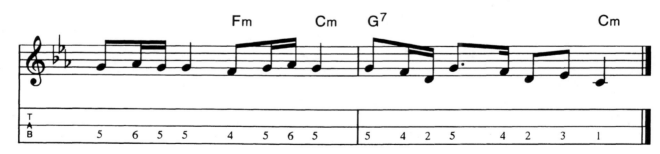

An Dro
from Arzh

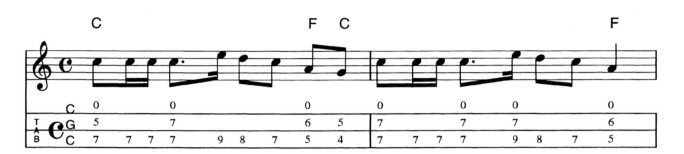

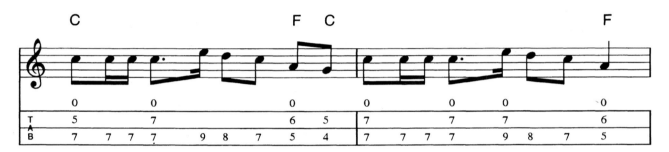

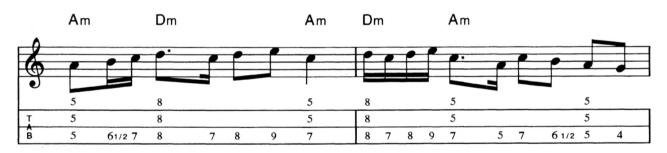

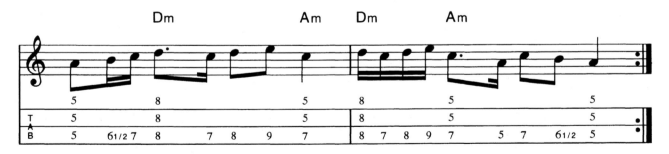

Plin

Mael-Pestiven

Jabadaw

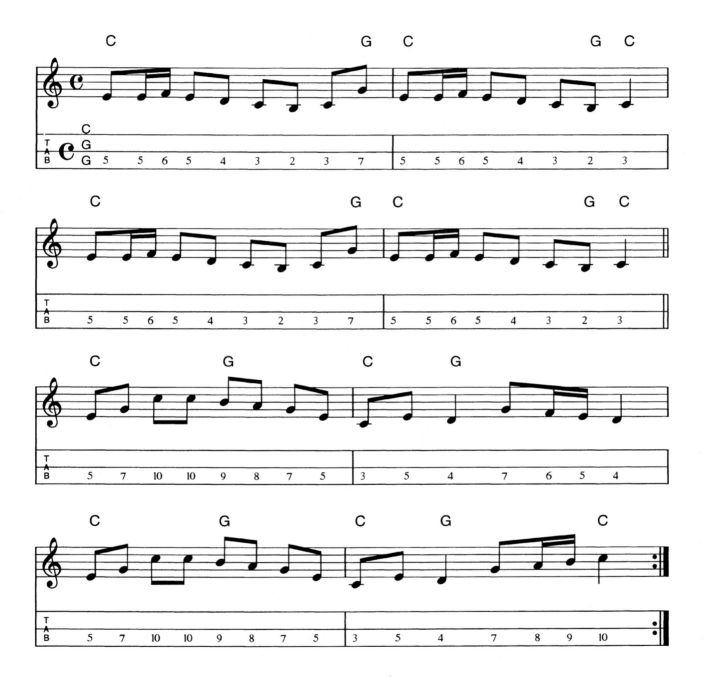

155

Breton March

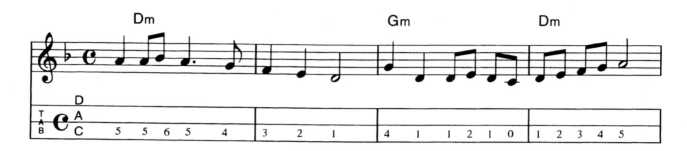

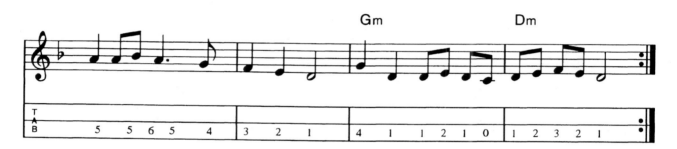

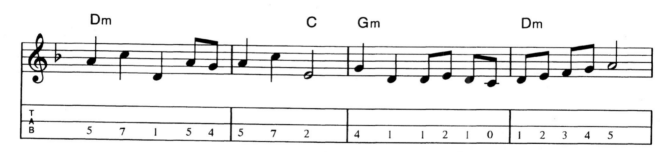

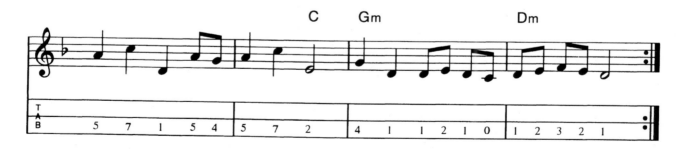

An Dro
from Baod

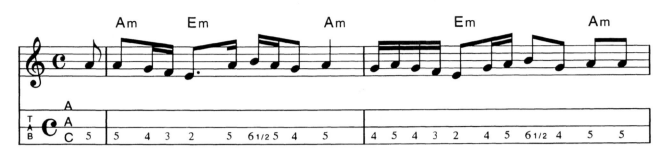

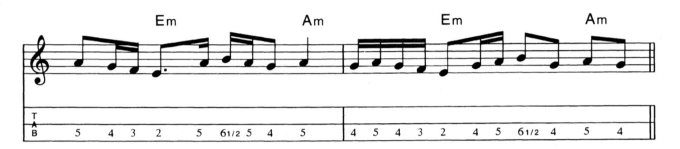

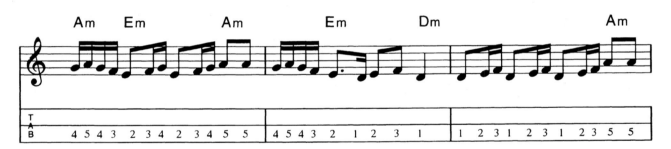

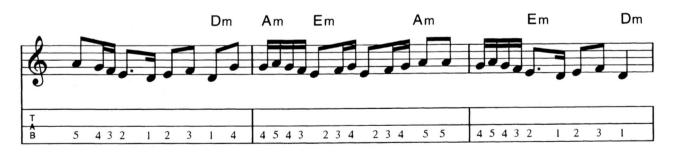

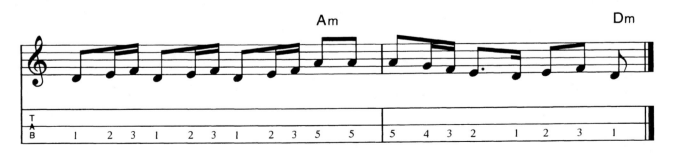

Danse Des Baguettes
Two Breton Dances

#1

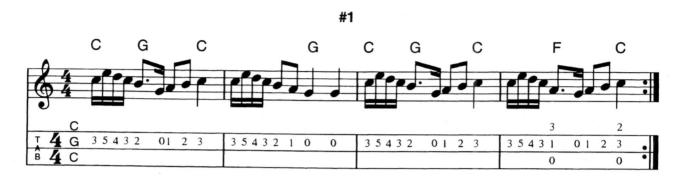

#2

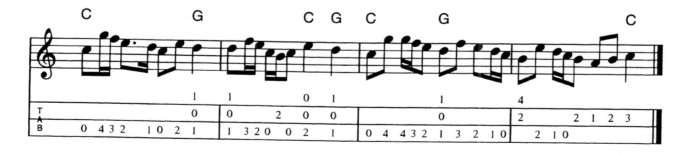

Laridenn
Pluergad

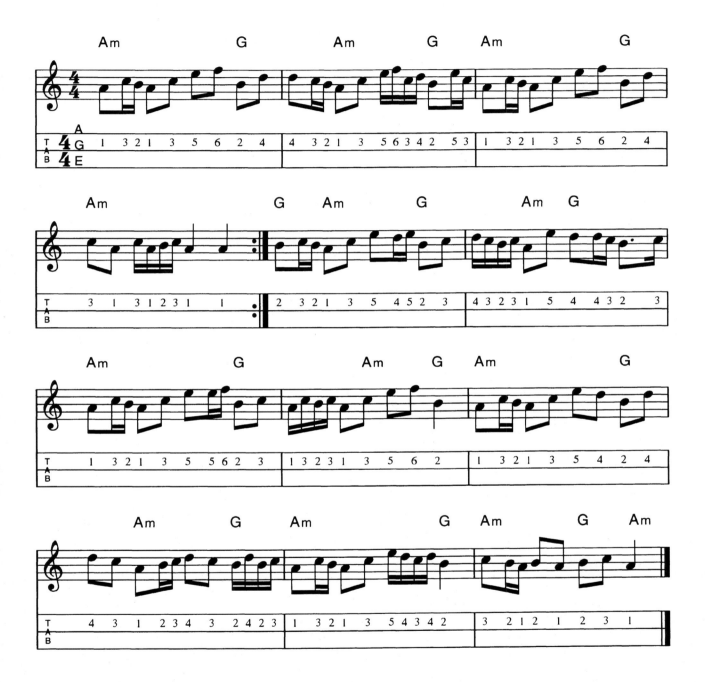

159

An Dro
Plenweur

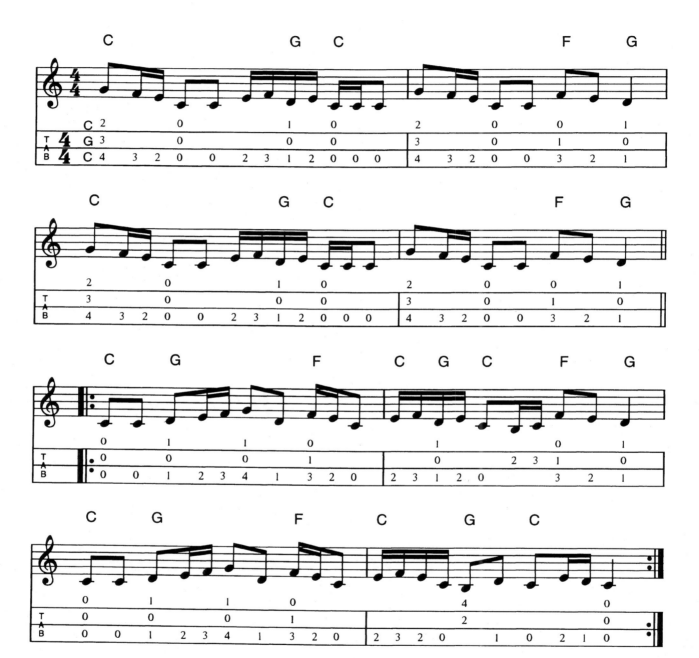

Hanter-Dro

Pluergad

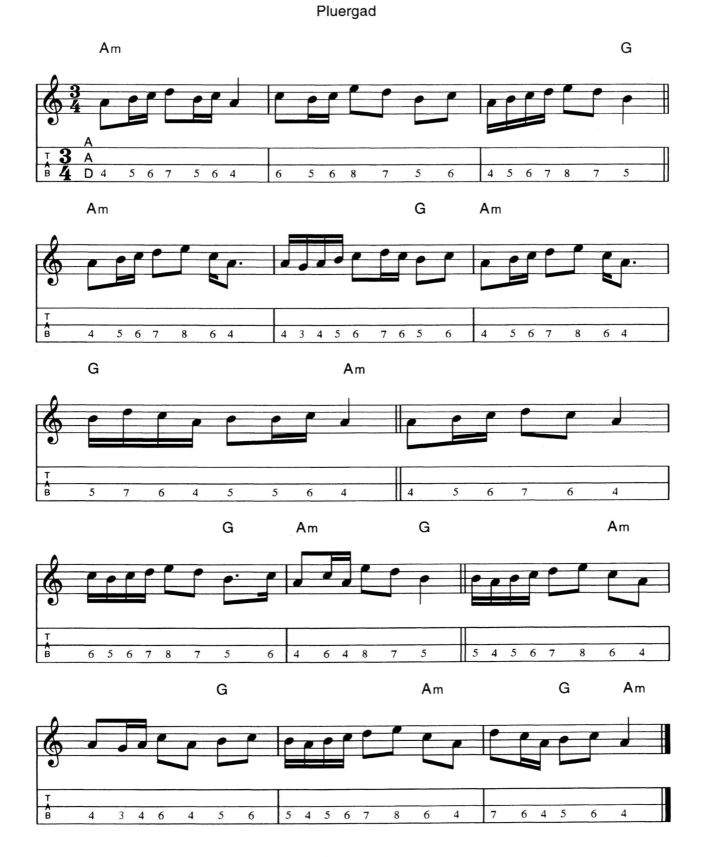

161

Voici Venir le Joli Mois de Mai
Song

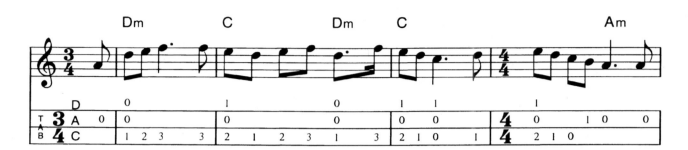

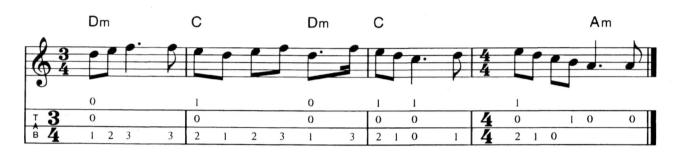

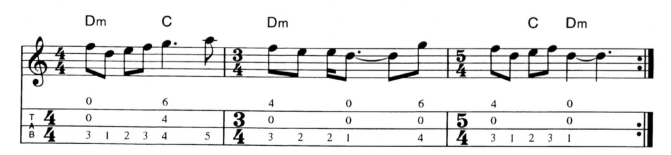

About the Author

Mark Nelson has played Celtic music on the dulcimer right from the start; the first tune he picked out on his newly-completed dulcimer back in 1969 was the *Skye Boat Song!* After several years of playing old time, Irish and Scottish music in various bands in Utah, he toured in England and Ireland in the summer of 1975, playing in theaters, pubs and street corners and picking up tunes from outstanding traditional musicians.

Since that time he has continued to expand his knowledge and love of traditional music on the dulcimer and other instruments. A former Winfield dulcimer champion, he has recorded numerous albums and authored several instructional books and video tapes. He has appeared at festivals, colleges, workshops and concerts across the United States and Canada---from Barrow to Boston and everywhere in between.

He lives in Southern Oregon's Applegate Valley, where he divides his time between music, writing and keeping the dogs amused.

Author's Discography

Numerous Celtic tunes, including many of the tunes in this book may be found on the following albums (only the tunes of Celtic origin are listed):

"The Rights of Man—Fiddle tunes for Dulcimer" Kicking Mule Records KM 218
> Barney Brallaghan
> Campbell's Farewell to Red Castle (as "Campbell's Farewell to Red Gap")
> The Cork March
> The Duke of Fife
> Farewell to Whiskey
> Paddy on the Railroad
> Off to California
> Hewlett
> Petronella
> The Rights of Man
> The Road to Lisdoonvarna

"After the Morning (Irish, Scottish and American Music for Dulcimer)" Kicking Mule records KM 241
> An Comhra Dunn
> The Boys of Ballisodare
> Delahunty's Hornpipe
> Earl's Chair
> Joe O'Dowd's Jig
> The Joys of My Life
> The Kid on the Mountain
> Morrison's Jig
> The Kesh Jig
> My Home
> Planxty Irwin

"Winfield Champions" Wood 'n' Strings Records #104. Wood n' Strings, 1513 Baker Rd., Burleson, TX 76028
> The Frost is All Over
> The Rose in the Heather

"Southern Light" Flying Fish Records #405
> The Boys of Wexford (as "Under Dogwood")

"Waves of Light" Acme Arts, PO Box 967, Jacksonville, OR 97530.
> Si Beg Si Mor (as "The Faery Hills")

"Autumn." Music for solo dulcimer and guitar. Acme Arts, PO Box 967, Jacksonville, OR 97530.
> Hugh O'Donnell
> The Downfall of Paris

Other albums, books and videos:

"The Dulcimer Workshop" Instruction Series. Book and Six One Hour Cassettes. Kicking Mule Records.

"21 Fiddle Tunes" Book with Cassette. Kicking Mule Records.

"Beginning Appalachian Dulcimer" Instructional video. Lark in The Morning Video, distributed by Mel Bay Publications.

"Dynamic Dulcimer" Instructional video with many international tunes. Lark in The Morning Video, distributed by Mel Bay Publications.

"Making Homemade Instruments" Instructional video. Lark in The Morning Video, distributed by Mel Bay Publications.

"You Can Teach Yourself to Make Homemade Musical Instruments" Book and Cassette tape or CD, includes plans to build a tin can dulcimer. Mel Bay Publications.

Mark Nelson may be contacted % **Acme Arts, P.O. Box 967, Jacksonville, OR 97530.**

Alphabetical Index of Tunes